MARY MOODY has been a prolific gardening author and a former presenter on ABC TV's 'Gardening Australia'. Her books include *The Good Life* (1995), *A Gardener's Companion* (2001), *Au Revoir* (2001) and *Last Tango in Toulouse* (2003). Mary divides her year between her farm near Bathurst in New South Wales, and her house in south-west France.

Also by Mary Moody

Au Revoir
Last Tango in Toulouse

THE
LONG HOT
SUMMER

THE LONG HOT SUMMER

A French heatwave and a marriage meltdown

MARY MOODY

MACMILLAN

Pan Macmillan Australia

First published 2005 in Macmillan by Pan Macmillan Australia Pty Limited
St Martins Tower, 31 Market Street, Sydney

National Library of Australia
Cataloguing-in-Publication data:

Moody, Mary, 1950– .
The long hot Summer: a French heatwave and a
marriage meltdown.

ISBN 1 40503670 2.

1. Moody, Mary, 1950– . 2. Disasters – Social aspects. 3.
Heat waves (Meteorology) – France. 4. Marriage. I. Title.

363.34921

Set in 11.5/16 pt New Baskerville by Midland Typesetters
Printed in Australia by McPherson's Printing Group

INTRODUCTION

If I were a poet or a novelist, writing this book would be less difficult. I could fictionalise the main characters to maintain their anonymity. I could set the narrative in a different place and a different time, and in doing so protect myself from publicly acknowledging that the story I am writing is my own. It is a dangerous business, writing about your own life in such a personal, revealing way without exposing yourself to public criticism by appearing self-absorbed.

It's now four years since I ran away from my real life in search of a quiet time for reflection. It was the year I turned fifty, and I seized upon a brief window of opportunity for escape. Our children had grown up, left home and were well established – indeed I already had the delight of four grandchildren. My mother, who had lived with us for twenty-five years, had died suddenly and my career, although demanding, could easily be put on hold – for a little while at least.

That first year I spent six months living alone in a small room at the back of a shop in a medieval village in a remote rural region of France called the Lot. It was the first time I had ever lived alone and I revelled in the delights of that first long, hot summer with its village fairs and markets and days filled with socialising and sightseeing and balmy twilights where the sun doesn't set until nearly eleven at night. I fell in love with France and ended up buying a small house in a nearby village with the full support of my husband David, who had remained in Australia for the six months of my escape to work on two feature films being shot in Queensland. When he realised how serious I was about wanting to buy a house in France, David flew over for the last few weeks of my stay so that we could choose the perfect place together.

It's a modest house with enormous charm in the quaint village of Frayssinet-le-Gelat, which is surrounded by fields of maize and dense oak and chestnut woodlands. For me, the decision to buy a French property was made with a sense of urgency because I was worried that after going home my life would just revert to its usual round of deadlines and demands. I feared that the personal gains I had made by living alone, immersed in a different and fascinating culture, would rapidly disappear. It's like when you say goodbye at the end of a much-loved holiday, always expecting to return some day. But I knew in my heart that I would get caught up in the pressures of my life and never find time to go back to this unique region that had won my heart. By buying a house there would be a permanent connection. A reason to return year after year.

If David had been able to foresee then how buying a house in France would so dramatically change our lives, I am positive he would never have agreed. Indeed, he has said just that many times as we've struggled to remain together through the tumultuous events that have unfolded.

Each year I go back to France with a purpose. I need a place where I can be my own person and have some time out from the usual demands of my life, but I am also taking refuge to write and just be alone if I choose to be. Or socialise non-stop if that's what my heart desires. My way of justifying the time to myself and the expense of having a bolt hole so far from home is to organise village walking tours. Each year I lead a small group from Australia and introduce them to the delights of this little-known historic region. It's a lot of fun but it also takes a lot of energy so I spend some time, both before and after each tour, chilling out in our village house.

Since buying the house I have written two books about my travels and adventures – *Au Revoir* (2001) and *Last Tango in Toulouse* (2003) – and they have received a very mixed reception. The books are not simply travelogues that detail where I go and who I meet and what I see. I do write about Frayssinet-le-Gelat and our house renovations and the wonderful local food and wine, but the books are about much more than that. They are an intensely personal journal in which I take a long hard look at my life, past and present. I openly discuss the problems of long-term relationships, including my own thirty-three year marriage. I describe the delights of living alone for the first time and the difficulties of confronting the menopause and the inevitable ageing process. I write openly about the unexpected sexual drive that some women experience at this age and I ponder on what I really want to do with the rest of my life.

After the publication of my last book some readers objected to such a candid memoir. While I accept that some may distrust my motives for throwing into the public arena events that many people regard as strictly personal, I maintain my right to document the difficult and often painful journey I've been on these last few years. Those who object, I am sure, strongly identify and sympathise with my husband, who is an integral part of my life and has therefore unwittingly become a character in my books. There's no doubt that the subjects I touch on in my writing are often confronting and painful for David, but although he would prefer that I wasn't so candid at times, he nevertheless supports my right to express my feelings – provided that I do not misrepresent his point of view.

For me, writing is a form of therapy, a way of crystallising the events and making some sense of them. It can be therapeutic for David at times, too. He read and reread the last book – far more often than I have – as a way of trying to gain some insight into what I struggled to express.

Yet I am painfully aware that writing 'warts and all' about my life while I am in the midst of living it is a totally bizarre situation. Often it feels unreal to me. Until all this happened I was a journalist who had made a successful career as a gardening writer and television presenter. After the publication of *Au Revoir*, which was part memoir and part travelogue, my writing career took a turn in a totally different direction. Instead of inspiring gardeners with the joys of making compost, I find myself writing about drinking too much red wine at lunch and being stopped by the gendarmes while driving back to my little French village. Instead of telling people how I go about pruning my roses, I'm describing how I fell in love and had an affair.

When *Last Tango in Toulouse* was published the reaction was fairly divided. On the one hand I was applauded for being 'honest and brave' by many of my readers, those who empathised with the various dilemmas and contradictions I was facing. These readers, who came to my literary lunches and bookshop events, wrote me the most encouraging and supportive letters and they seemed to understand – or at least appreciate – my way of dealing with the problems I was facing in my life. Of the rest, many had not actually read the book but instead reacted adversely to the publicity surrounding its publication. As a result, some determined that I was totally selfish. It was certainly difficult reading some of those negative reviews and comments, but I couldn't allow myself to be overly concerned about what other people thought of me, especially strangers. Doing so can be almost as dangerous as believing your own publicity.

In a sense I am caught on a treadmill. Having tried so hard to escape one set of demands and commitments, I find myself caught up in another equally demanding life and career. There is little I can do but continue living my life and writing about it as I go, while ever hopeful that sometime soon a sense of normality will return. At times it seems unlikely.

Mary Moody,
March 2005

1

How did I find myself in such a weird situation, confessing my misdeeds in print in the book *Last Tango in Toulouse*? It was never planned, it just evolved. After the success of *Au Revoir* I signed a contract with my publishers to write a second book about my travels and adventures in France. While I was flattered at being asked to continue telling my story, I was also a little nervous that there wouldn't be enough fresh material to sustain an interesting narrative. The feedback from the first book had been very positive and although I wasn't approaching the second book as a 'sequel', I realised that I had to write in the same voice and with the same enthusiasm as the first one because it had resonated so well with the readers. At the time of signing the contract, I remember making an offhand remark to my publisher and my agent, and ironically also to David, that I should probably have some raunchy sex in the new book to add some sparkle to the plot. An affair, or even a couple of affairs. That would liven up proceedings. We all laughed.

In mid-2002 I launched myself into writing the new book with more confidence about the structure and the way the narrative should flow, with overlapping chapters set in France and back home in Australia. David and I were now living on a farm at Yetholme, near Bathurst, and gradually starting to get more organised and acclimatised to country living. For twenty-five years, while our children were growing up, we had lived in the Blue Mountains, and although we had a large garden it was never as much work as the acreage we were now trying to maintain. At my instigation we had started breeding geese and ducks, and David surprised me by taking on the role of goose-herder with great enthusiasm. He fussed over the birds, rounding them up every evening to lock them away from the foxes, and became so attached to our first batch of goslings that I feared we would never have the heart to kill and eat them.

Water on the farm was an ongoing problem, and we continued to battle the workings of our water pump and household plumbing. We are fortunate to have a deep spring to supply the house and garden with a seemingly unending flow of water, but it needs to be pumped up from a paddock which is two hundred metres behind the old farm sheds. There were many days when David would turn on the tap first thing in the morning to put the kettle on for tea and not one drop would emerge. I have since discovered that this sort of situation is par for the course on rural properties. But my husband is not a handyman, and although he would do his best to track down the problem – usually a burst pipe somewhere underground between the spring and house – inevitably we had to send for help from the local water contractors. It was all costing a small fortune, and when we looked at our overall expenditure we realised that our dream of living on a farm was proving to be very costly indeed. And that, combined with the cost of owning a house in France, was putting us under considerable financial pressure. So while David tried to keep on top of the farm management while also developing his various filmmaking projects, I set about starting work on the second book.

Writing has become a way of life for me. I developed disciplined working habits back in the late sixties when I trained as a journalist. Newspaper and magazine offices are busy, noisy places and I quickly adopted a technique of being able to write fast and meet deadlines in spite of the endless noise and clatter of ringing phones, loud conversations and multiple other distractions. It was critical to success as a journalist. Only the star writers and columnists had quiet rooms of their own in which to write; the rest of us produced our copy in open-plan offices which were noisy and smoky but also lots of fun. I delighted in the camaraderie and the buzzy atmosphere, where the deadline was paramount but the tension was alleviated by the good spirits of my fellow workers.

During the decades I worked as a gardening writer, I managed to fit the demanding deadlines in and around my hectic home life. I had four growing children and a large house and garden to care for. I structured my day around writing and started in the early morning in the hope that my mind would be sharper. The plan was to finish by lunchtime so I could spend the rest of the day gardening, have time with the children after school and then prepare the family dinner. I quickly realised that if I allowed my disciplined routine to lapse the family would suffer. I would be fraught and bad-tempered as the deadline approached. So I stuck to my regime to maintain family harmony.

To get started on this new book I decided to write about recent events in our lives: our problems adapting to rural life; the tragic death of our farming neighbour Russell in a road accident; and the joyful arrival of our fifth grandson, Augustus James, who was born on my birthday in June. The writing came easily and I started to feel confident that I could produce another book with the same honesty as *Au Revoir*.

Not long into the writing, the time came for me to pack up and fly to France, where I was to meet up with our youngest son Ethan and his partner Lynne, now heavily pregnant, who had been living in our village house for six months to experience the lifestyle and also to start work on some much needed painting and renovating. Ethan and Lynne were about to return to Australia to have their baby and I wanted to spend a week or so with them before having some precious time alone in the house. This was my first return visit to the region after the life-changing six months I had written about in *Au Revoir* and I was filled with excitement and anticipation. I would have the chance to live in the house for the first time as a local rather than just being a visitor, and I was thrilled at the prospect of catching up with all the friends I had made the previous summer.

Since buying the house I had agonised about how to organise a legitimate way of living part of each year in France, not, as I had done the previous year, as an extended holiday, but involved in some sort of business that would generate income. I had given up my television job on 'Gardening Australia' and I desperately needed to replace it with an alternative career. Writing memoirs wouldn't be enough to sustain houses in two countries.

The plan I came up with was to organise small tour groups of Australians to visit the region. So this first return visit was primarily to set up an interesting itinerary that would include several hours of walking every day, visits to historic villages, châteaux and gardens, plus lots of regional restaurant meals. Doing the research for the tour would be fun and I decided to work with my New Zealand-born friend Jan Claudy as co-guide and translator.

I was thrilled to be back. The villagers greeted me warmly and my wide circle of friends embraced me with delight. Lunches and dinners and sight-seeing expeditions of the region filled my days and evenings with fun, and I wondered how I was ever going to settle back into farm life in Bathurst after another dose of southwest France.

Then something happened that changed everything. Forever.

While balancing the mix of work and pleasure, I stumbled into the early stages of the relationship with the man with whom I would have a passionate affair the following year – the man from Toulouse. Although at this stage the relationship was not physical, it hit me like a bolt out of the blue and I was deeply disturbed by what had been stirred inside me. My mental confusion was so apparent, even at that embryonic stage, that when I returned to Australia at the end of the month-long visit David instantly recognised the first signs that there were rocky times ahead.

So unsettled was my state of mind that I sought professional counselling for the first time in my life and, as I picked up the threads of writing the book, I decided to document the way I was feeling, because the act of accepting outside help was for me a huge admission of vulnerability. All my life I had coped with problems and challenges on my own. My unsettled early childhood, the ups and downs of my marriage, dealing with my ageing live-in mother and the trials and tribulations of rearing four teenage children with a frequently absent, work-obsessed husband. I had become smug about my ability to handle the rough with the smooth, so it was only natural that I would be rattled by confronting a situation over which I felt I had absolutely no control.

At this time I decided to speak to my publisher and confide in him that I didn't know how I was going to deal with the writing of this next book. I wasn't confident I could continue writing it at all. I explained, without giving away too much detail, that my life was in a state of emotional turmoil and that there was a possibility that my seemingly stable marriage might be about to crumble around me. How could I write a happy, upbeat book about my midlife adventures in France when my life as I knew it was falling apart?

This eight-month period between when I came back from France in October with the possibility of a love affair looming and when I returned the following May to lead a garden tour was the most troubled in our lives. Knowing that there had been a huge emotional shift, David and I established an intimacy and intensity in our relationship that we hadn't experienced in years. It was as if there was a sword dangling over our marriage. Writing the book became almost impossible, and I wondered how I would ever meet the deadline at the end of the year. And what would I write about? How could I produce an honest and credible account of this phase of my life if there was a dark secret I was unable to include as part of the story?

After the garden tour of France and England I went back to Frayssinet and recklessly launched myself into the love affair that had been smouldering in the background. David briefly came to stay after his annual trip to the Cannes Film Festival and it was obvious to him from the moment he arrived that what he had feared since last year had actually transpired. He said nothing at the time, but waited until I came home in July to confront me with his certainty of my infidelity. It was a nightmare.

As if dealing with the ramifications of the affair wasn't enough to contend with, we also had to grapple with the issue of the book I was supposed to be writing. While we were struggling to repair our damaged relationship, the situation was compounded by the prospect of a book that would add further pain to our fragile state of mind. I argued that if it was to be written at all, the book must be totally honest to ring true with the readers. But David believed that this major crisis in our lives was deeply personal and therefore should not be included in my story.

That same September I returned to France to lead the village walking tour that had been twelve months in the planning. The agreement I made with David was that I should meet briefly with my lover in Toulouse and end the affair. This I did, and despite the intense pain I experienced ending what had been such a significant relationship, I hoped it would be enough to salvage my marriage. Then two unexpected and quite overwhelming events intervened. Just when I thought I was getting my life back on track, it went even more haywire. The events were sexual and in many ways quite shocking, and I knew that the only way I could survive was to keep them completely secret from David. Our relationship, which even at its most troubled had been open and honest, was now to become one of lies and deceit.

After the walking tour I returned to Australia and was left with just a few months to finish writing the book. David and I were constantly at each other's throats debating the rights and wrongs of how the story should be told.

'It's difficult enough dealing with what's happened in our marriage,' David would storm. 'But including it all in a book will make it ten times worse. It will never end, it will just keep coming back to haunt us. What will it be like when the book comes out? The publicity? The reviews?'

I was overwhelmed with frustration and confusion. I couldn't see how I could simply ignore or skim over an event that was so fundamental to the narrative. The readers would expect an honest account of my journey through mid-life, no matter how rocky. Yet I knew I had already hurt David deeply, and writing the story in a book would drag that pain into the future.

As the deadline approached I became more and more agitated over my inability to articulate on the page. This was a situation I had never encountered before. Writing had always come easily to me, but this time every hour spent at the computer was pure agony. Our usually joyful family Christmas came and went, much more strained than usual, and I had less than a month to hand over the manuscript.

David hovered nervously around the house, popping in and out of my office and asking me constantly how the writing was going. Well, it wasn't going anywhere. I was going round and round in circles – writing all sorts of trivial side stories to avoid tackling what had become the central issue.

One morning I sat at the keyboard and decided that the only way ahead was to write openly about my affair with the man from Toulouse. Not in any graphic sexual detail, but just how it felt. I tried desperately in my writing to pinpoint the emotional aspects of this unexpected and passionate relationship. The anticipation, the fear, the excitement, the intensity, the love – and then the pain of the abrupt ending. It was barely four pages. I gave it to David to read and his response was shattering. Seeing it on the page was even more distressing than all the soul-searching conversations we had been through as I struggled to explain the way I was feeling. For me, the writing had been cathartic. We spent days and days in tears, sometimes shouting at each other, sometimes holding each other close. We often fell into bed for the afternoon, clinging to each other, exhausted by the process. Nothing was resolved.

Three weeks before the deadline I knew the book would never be finished in time at the rate I was going. David was adamant that what I had written about the affair could not be woven into the book. I, on the other hand, believed it was an essential part of my story. We reached a stalemate.

I am phobic about deadlines after years and years of working as a journalist, and my mood darkened daily as I realised I had written myself into a corner. David went into Bathurst every day to the gym, and one morning I watched from my office window as his car disappeared down the long drive and out towards the highway. The computer screen sat blankly staring at me. I knew I had to get out.

I drove my ute – the farm vehicle – around to the front door and unplugged my computer. It's a huge, awkward collection of equipment, including a 45-centimetre screen, and weighs a tonne. I lugged it bit by bit out to the car and strapped it into the front seat, hoping that I would manage to reassemble it correctly when I reached my destination. Not that I knew where I was going, just that I had to find a quiet place, away from all possible distractions, to finish my story.

I threw a few clothes into a bag and headed off, leaving a message for David on his mobile phone message bank: 'When you get back from town I won't be here. Don't worry, I haven't run away again. I just need to go somewhere where I can finish the book in peace. I'll phone you when I'm settled. Love you, bye.'

I drove gingerly towards Lithgow with the computer bouncing wildly on the front seat because the ute has bad suspension. I started to worry that the journey might damage the hard drive – then what would I do? The book would be lost, as in my harried state I hadn't thought to back up the manuscript before I left. But in a funny way I thought losing the book at this stage mightn't be such a bad thing. It would certainly eliminate the impasse between me and my husband.

In Lithgow I started investigating motels but quickly discovered they were all booked out. It was during the January bushfires and visiting fire-fighters had taken over every room. Not wanting to go to the mountains, I took a right turn and headed towards Oberon. The road was really bumpy – almost a dirt track in places – and the computer was having a very rough ride indeed. The first motel on the left as I drove into town had a huge, ugly fish, at least five metres high, positioned near the entrance. It was called 'The Big Trout Motor Inn' and I suppose was intended to attract the custom of fishermen who come to the region for the excellent fly fishing. I booked a room for two weeks, nervously reconnected the computer cables and plugged in the telephone wire in the hope of being able to send emails.

I held my breath as I switched the computer on, but to my great relief it all worked perfectly. Even the internet connected. The first thing I did was to send a copy of the existing manuscript to my email address, where it could be retrieved should anything go wrong with the computer.

The rooms at the Big Trout are large and comfortable and air-conditioned, which was a godsend in the stifling heat of that particular January. Fortunately there was also a large round table capable of accommodating my computer and all the various print-outs of the manuscript. I set myself up with some basic groceries so that I wouldn't need to leave the room during the day. I really wanted to maximise the amount of work I could achieve in the short time left to me. The owners probably thought I was eccentric. I refused housekeeping and locked myself away like a recluse with the curtains drawn and only the hum of my computer's hard drive for company. I told them I would accept phone calls but none came through. Nobody really knew where I was, which suited me fine.

I started to write in earnest. Without the distractions of the farm and the pressure I felt from David's discomfort at the content of the book, it flowed from my fingertips at an alarming rate. I established a routine of getting up early and writing for three hours in my nightdress, with several cups of tea to sustain me. I then showered, made my own breakfast and continued to write for another three hours or more. I made a light lunch in my room and lay down for an hour to sleep or read. I wrote again all afternoon until hunger started to distract me, and then I went out for the first and only time of the day. Up to the local pub for a steak sandwich and a beer or two.

It was a blissful existence requiring no effort apart from the creative process of writing. For the first time I could appreciate why so many writers find it impossible to concentrate with all the distractions of home. While I could easily bash out a gardening book with kids creating havoc all around me, when it came to writing in a deeper emotional sense I needed absolute peace and quiet. The Big Trout Motor Inn, phoney fish and all, was my haven.

I phoned David to tell him where I was and to reassure him I was safe. I also told him I was doing my best to write the book without any reference to the love affair. I painstakingly removed all references to it in the manuscript, and tried to flesh out other aspects of my travels instead. David sounded relieved, and surprisingly wasn't at all fazed by my sudden disappearance. He even offered to come over one evening and take me out for a meal. Which he did, and we had a very relaxed, stress-free evening together. Better than we had managed in months.

The rest of the time in Oberon I ate alone, watching the TV news over the bar in the local pub. I didn't stay more than an hour because by early evening I was totally wrung out by the volume of writing I had done – sometimes up to 5,000 words a day. One evening two rather ragged-looking blokes were sitting in the bar as I ate my toasted sandwich. In their mid-thirties, they were a scruffy pair with gnarled hands, more than a few teeth missing and hair that appeared not to have been washed or brushed for weeks. I took them to be timber workers, as Oberon is a big forestry region, and I also gathered that they had probably been in the pub all day because they were past the point of coherence. One called out to me.

'Gidday luv, ow'ya goin'?'

'Fine,' I said, continuing to eat and watch the news.

'You know somethin', luv,' he continued, 'you look great.'

'Thanks,' I said, thinking I should probably down my beer quickly and leave.

'If anyone tells you that you don't look great, luv, don't you believe them. Because you look great,' he went on, trying to win me over with his backhanded compliment.

He then staggered around the bar and stood close, far too close for comfort, pressing his snaggle-toothed, beery mouth to my ear.

'You know somethin', luv,' he said, grinning broadly. 'You could do better than me.'

I stifled a laugh and responded, 'You know something, I probably could,' bolting my sandwich and making a hasty retreat, laughing at his self-deprecating, clumsy pick-up line that for me was quintessential Australian male. I don't know how he thought I would respond, but probably not quite the way I did.

3

After nearly two weeks of frenetic writing the book had evolved to a stage where it was virtually complete. I had carefully gone through and removed all reference to the love affair. I hoped instead that the chapters I had written about the joy and excitement of finding my sister Margaret after a separation of nearly fifty years would give the book the emotional resonance it needed. I had written about this extraordinary tale of family separation in *Au Revoir* when I described my early childhood with alcoholic parents, and my half-sister who left our dysfunctional home and never returned. After the book was released, a reader contacted me with information on Margaret's whereabouts in Canada, and I was able to contact her and then visit her in person. It was the happiest of reunions, and I told the story in the new book.

I curled up on the hotel bed and started to read through the entire manuscript from where I had begun writing more than twelve months before.

It's very difficult reading back over your own work and I often avoid doing so unless pressured into it by a persistent editor. But it was essential to get a feeling for the book as whole, so I set aside time just for reviewing it all. As I turned the pages I realised that what I had written had a hollow ring to it. It just didn't make sense. The central character, me, was in a state of turmoil. My distress and confusion were obvious but there was little explanation for this, other than my menopausal condition and my questioning of my long-term relationship with my husband. I found the narrative deeply unsatisfying, and knew that anyone reading this book would feel as though they had been left dangling. I knew at that moment I had to tell the rest of story, no matter how painful. All or nothing. I returned to the computer and sat through the night reinstating the sections pertaining to the affair.

Then I phoned David and told him of my change of heart.

'I think you'd better come home now,' he said.

So I packed up my belongings – having first emailed myself the finished manuscript as a back-up – and drove the bumpy one hour back to Yetholme. It was lovely to be home, although the paddocks were bleached white from the hot dry winds and one dam had completely dried up. The bushfires that had been raging in the region had not come close this time, but the potential was always there, the farm being surrounded by pine forests and remnants of native vegetation.

I returned the computer to my office desk, hooked it up to the printer, then printed out the five hundred or so pages for David to read.

It was a gut-churning day and a half. He sat in the back room drinking wine and smoking cigars while he methodically read through the book. Sometimes I'd hear him laugh, which was a great relief. But then he'd go quiet for what seemed like hours at a time. It was nail-biting.

Eventually he emerged and handed me back the well-thumbed pages.

'It's an amazing book,' he said. 'Very honest, very funny, very sad. But I'm never going to like it. To be quite honest, I hate it. But I totally support your right to write about your life and what has been happening to you these last few years.'

That was it. I hugged him but he stiffened under my embrace. He was still deeply hurt and traumatised by the events of the last year. But he wouldn't stand in my way.

He had flagged various pages in the text where he had concerns and together we worked to tidy up the final draft. Then to further demonstrate his support he actually delivered the final printed-out copies to the publisher's Sydney offices. On deadline, double-spaced, with the pages tied together with red satin ribbon.

My relief at getting the book finished while not destroying my marriage at the same time was palpable. I thought our troubles had finished, but they were only just beginning.

4

 My life has always been a juggling act. As a child I tried to juggle the unpredictable emotions of my unstable parents and from an early age developed all sorts of strategies for maintaining family harmony. I found that by being bright and cheerful, amusing and helpful, I could defuse family tensions and keep life on a more even keel. I carried these techniques for handling difficult situations into adulthood and they have certainly come in very handy during my complex life. I juggled a demanding career while rearing four children and managed that most delicate of tightrope acts, negotiating good relations in an extended family that included my career-driven husband and my hard-drinking and frequently difficult mother.

Now, if it's possible, I have created an even more complicated and anxiety-ridden existence for myself at an age when my life should, by rights, be starting to become more relaxed and easier to manage. I have split myself in half. I am trying to lead a double life. When I am in France I am one woman: independent, free-spirited, impulsive, self-indulgent, outspoken, wilful, at times wild and irresponsible. Reckless. I love this new person because in many ways she is the real me who has been trying to get out for years. Aspects of this hidden me have always been obvious to my close friends and family, but they have been outweighed by the other half of me, the responsible and hard-working one. The wife and mother, the daughter and the grandmother. The backbone of the family. The matriarch.

Now I am endeavouring to achieve what I fear is impossible. I am trying to hang on to my husband and our family life while still relishing the freedom I experience when living in France. I don't wish to exclude David from being part of both my worlds, but I do want to have a little time in France on my own to write, to lead my walking tours and to be enveloped by the glorious sensation of being 'me' which I have only ever experienced when I am in the village on my own. When I am in France, Australia seems like a dream. I miss my children and even more so my grandchildren, but I know that they are getting on extremely well without me. I also know that I will return to them soon – I will always return to my home and my family, and this makes the separations much easier to bear.

As for David, I have grown accustomed over many years to living apart from him for long periods and I have always believed it to be quite a healthy thing for our relationship. Now that he is working from home at the farm, I find that being able to escape for a while to France is maintaining that balance in our lives. We can go our separate ways and meet up again, whether in France or back at the farm. It seems like the perfect arrangement.

My friends claim jealously that I have achieved 'the perfect life'. A house in France, time alone, a place in the Australian countryside, a warm and loving family and a devoted husband.

But I know this is far, far from the truth. I am struggling to maintain the facade of this dream and I know that it must eventually collapse around me because it is nothing more than a facade. A front. The truth is much less palatable.

5

 I have never been a nervous woman. In all my years of travel I have only ever taken the simplest security precautions with my travel documents, money and passport. I have wandered on my own through the back streets of New York, down laneways in New Delhi, and I even breached security regulations to explore Soweto when working on the feature film *Mapantsula* with David in the troubled city of Johannesburg in the late 1980s. I have never experienced a house robbery, car theft or bag-snatching, except for an odd incident when I was pregnant with our first child and living in Sydney. Two strange men wandered in through the front door of our semi-detached cottage in Crows Nest. Our family dog Wombat puffed himself up to double his usual border collie size and chased the strangers out the front gate. I easily dismissed that incident as a one-off and it didn't motivate me to remember to lock the car when I went shopping or the back door when I went to bed, even when David was away filming. It's a rather cavalier attitude to security which some people may regard as naïve or even reckless.

My mother Muriel, on the other hand, was always highly nervous and hated being left alone at night or even for long periods during the day. I'll never forget an incident that happened when Mum was well into her seventies. She was vacuuming the floor and was suddenly aware of someone at the glass doors of the front verandah. She turned off the cleaner and opened the door only to be confronted with a young man who appeared, to Mum's instant alarm, to be reaching inside the zipper of his trousers. She slammed the door in his face and took off like lightning through the house, out the back door and down into the garden where she somehow effortlessly scaled a 1.5-metre fence into the neighbour's back yard. After raising the alarm, she returned to our house with the neighbour in tow only to discover a small group of puzzled people gathered outside on the footpath. Our neighbour approached them and told them what had just happened to Muriel, and it turned out that the young man, who was slightly mentally retarded, was door-knocking for a well-known charity. Just before Mum opened the door he realised that his zip wasn't properly closed and was trying to rectify the situation when she appeared, misinterpreted his intentions and reacted – or overreacted. She was not amused when I shrieked with laughter at her story, especially the mental image of her getting over the back fence at a stage of life when she found climbing the front stairs an effort.

I never wanted to be like Mum, frightened of my own shadow, so in some respects I almost consciously went in the other direction by totally disregarding the possibility of stranger danger. Over the years David has often remonstrated with me for my casual attitude to locking doors, and I have only become more conscious of the need to lock up the house, the sheds and cars since moving to the farm because, as he quite rightly points out, our insurance won't cover us if we are robbed when the locks aren't in use. But when living in France I tend to revert to my lackadaisical attitude to security, probably because I feel more like I'm on holiday than living in the real world. I try to remember to lock the house and car last thing at night, but during the day the downstairs shutters are wide open and the side door is always unlocked unless I am going to be out for the whole day.

There's a feeling of security living in the middle of the village, surrounded by neighbours, with people coming and going from the car park across the road. I don't even have curtains – my charming French doors and windows give me an uninterrupted view of the bustle of village life outside, and those who walk past have a clear view of my cosy living area both night and day. I don't feel vulnerable or exposed, I just feel like part of the life of the village.

When I first lived in France a few years ago, I rented a little cottage nestled deep in the woods for three months. My friend Margaret Barwick was horrified when she first visited.

'However will you sleep at night?' she asked. 'Won't you be terrified being on your own in such a lonely, isolated place?'

But I wasn't at all jittery. It never occurred to me that I could possibly be the target of a crime. I have to admit these days I am no longer quite so blasé.

One evening in the middle of my September walking tour, I joined a small group of friends at the bar across the road for a drink after a hectic day of running around organising my tour group. As usual I left the side door to the house closed but unlocked. The group included an Englishman I had met briefly several years before when he was staying with a friend who lives in a village nearby. He was down on another visit, again staying with his friend, and we spent a very pleasant couple of hours in a small group talking and drinking. Three in the group decided to have a light meal – a simple steak and chips – but because I had eaten a larger than usual lunch on the tour, I decided to wait for a while and perhaps have an omelette or boiled egg when I got home.

As darkness fell, I realised I was tired and probably should get an early night in preparation for the busy day ahead. We had all noticed that the visiting man had disappeared. Initially we thought he had gone to the toilet, but when he failed to reappear we just assumed he had decided to walk back to the place where he was staying several kilometres up the road. I thought little of it, said my goodbyes and went immediately home.

Inside the house was in darkness. I turned on the light to the stairwell and went upstairs to change into my comfortable pyjamas. I came down, switched on the light in the kitchen and started to fill the sink with hot water to wash the glasses and coffee cups left from several hours before when members of the tour group had come to have a look at the house. Suddenly, from the corner of my eye, I noticed a movement in the shadows on the other side of the room. I looked around and there was the missing man, obviously the worse for wear from drink. His demeanour was menacing.

'Ah, there you are,' I said, trying to sound bright and unfazed by his presence, even though it had given me quite a start. 'We all wondered where you'd got to. Shall I phone your friend and get him to pick you up? There's a big storm brewing. If you try walking back now, you'll get soaked.'

I was babbling nervously and moving towards the phone when he grabbed me.

'I'm staying here with you,' he said, trying to kiss me. He really was far more drunk than any of us had realised and I knew in that instant that I was in big trouble. I would have to talk him around and somehow get to the phone and get some help.

But it wasn't going to be easy. He started handling me very roughly, pulling at my pyjamas in an effort to get them off. I wrestled with him but kept talking all the time, trying to reason with him rather than putting up a full-scale fight. A gut feeling told me that if I started to scream I could be in even worse trouble. That he might try to silence me with his large meaty hands around my throat. So I just kept talking and trying to fend him off.

He was a big man, very heavy and quite strong. He couldn't be talked down or reasoned with, he was way beyond that. He forced me backwards against the wooden staircase and dragged off my pyjama pants. He was trying to get me up the stairs, and the more I resisted the more he pushed my back hard against the wooden stairs. I could feel the impact of them on my backbone as I wrestled with him. He then started to bite me on the neck and breasts and on my inner thighs. It was appalling and I feared that if he got me all the way up to the bedroom I wouldn't be able to fend him off.

Although I was very frightened of the predicament I found myself in, I was also somehow strangely calm. I wanted to maintain at least some level of control of the situation. If I panicked, things could escalate and go terribly wrong. So I just kept talking and reasoning, not pleading but trying to make him see that what he was doing was a terrible mistake. I sensed that he was starting to be worn down by the struggle, although

he persisted, pushing me step by step up to the second floor,
where he grappled me into the back bedroom and onto one of
the narrow single beds.

There was a moment as he lay heavily on top of me, pinning
me to the bed, that it occurred to me it would probably be safer
and easier to just let him do whatever it was he wanted to do to
me so I could hopefully then get rid of him. But the thought was
so repugnant that I immediately set it aside and continued trying
to calm him down and talk him around. He hadn't managed to
remove any of his own clothes and he seemed to be slowing
down a little, so I was hopeful that I might be able to somehow
get out from under him. Suddenly, nature intervened.

The storm that had been brewing to the east for several hours
suddenly hit the village with a vengeance. A huge gust of wind
must have come down the main street, knocking my large front
shutters from their fastenings. The resulting crashing sound was
like the front doors being broken down and was loud enough
and violent enough to make my attacker jump to his feet in
alarm. That was all it took for me to be off the bed and down the
stairs, naked from the waist down, and out the door into the
street. By now the wind was really howling and it had started to
rain heavily, so there was no one in the street to witness my
distraught state. The man followed, and once out in the street he
lost his power over me.

I screamed at him to get away from me. Now. Run. I don't
think my language was very polite. As he moved off, I ran back
into the house, locking the door quickly behind me. Through
the front shutters, which were flapping around wildly in the
wind, I could see him scurrying around the corner and out of
sight, in the general direction of the place where he was staying.

I immediately phoned his friend and, by now almost hysterical, managed to tell him what had happened.

'Stay where you are,' he said, 'and I'll call the gendarmes.'

'No, no, I don't want the police involved,' I sobbed. 'The language problems are just too great. I can't deal with it all, not in the middle of a tour with all those people depending on me. And I don't want people to know. I'm perfectly okay, really. Just a few bruises,' I tried to reassure him. 'Just get hold of him – he's on the road back to your place. And get rid of him. As far away as possible.'

I must have been in shock, but at the time I was simply over-whelmed with relief that I had escaped shaken but relatively unscathed. I dressed and when I knew it was safe – because my friend called to say he had found the man, who was now packing his bag before being taken to catch the next train from Cahors – I ventured outside to close up the shutters and shut out the world.

I sat for more than an hour shaking like a leaf and trying to make sense of what had happened. My friend arrived, having dropped the man at the station, and sat up with me for hours while I went over and over the story. Debriefing. Reassuring myself and him that I was okay.

My friend continued to debate the rights and wrongs of involving the police. He argued, quite rightly, that his now ex-friend was obviously mentally unstable and that he could easily do the same sort of thing to another woman. That he probably already had a history of violence and aggression towards women. But I was really in no fit state to make a reasoned or sensible decision either for myself or for future victims of this man. I realise now that it was irresponsible, but my instinct at the time was to protect myself by just closing down and trying to bury it somewhere deep inside my psyche. I reasoned that if I could just get through the next few days I would be fine. That I was a strong woman, used to coping with difficulties. This was just another one and I would get through it.

I now understand why victims of rape often don't report the crime. It's a form of self-protection and a belief, often mistaken, that they will simply 'get over it'. But what happened to me didn't just disappear in a day or two, or even after a few weeks. I got up the following morning and was alarmed at the extent of the bruising and bite marks all over my body. But I showered, dressed and went on with my job as leader of the tour as though nothing had happened. Only Jan, who works side by side with me on the tours, twigged that something was amiss and when I finally told her, nervously, she was visibly shaken and very, very angry. She couldn't believe I hadn't called the gendarmes and gone to be examined at the hospital in Cahors. She wanted to send a group of local men to look for my attacker, but I assured her that he had long gone and was probably already out of the country. Or at least I hoped he was.

Thoughts of the attack haunted me for months, and although I didn't become a nervous wreck I certainly developed a habit of locking all the doors every time I left the house, even if I was just ducking around the corner to buy a loaf of bread from Sandrine in the boulangerie. One unpleasant result was the dreams I had, mostly harking back to the time I was raped in my teens. It had been my first sexual experience and certainly not a pleasant one, although I hadn't been as battered and bruised back then as I was this time around. But the memories of it, which hadn't disturbed me for many, many years, came flooding back and I realised that they had probably been buried just under the surface all that time. And that it takes a trigger like a second attack to stir up the fears and emotions once again. It made my flesh creep.

I also thought long and hard about my own behaviour and how it may easily have contributed to the situation. I know that it's not uncommon for women who are victims of sexual crime to blame themselves and I certainly don't believe that. But I do recognise that sitting around in bars drinking can put a woman at risk even if the people she's with are known to her. I didn't really know the man involved, but he was a friend of a friend, and I therefore assumed that he was fine. He was a known quantity. But he wasn't. He had a dark and violent aspect to his personality and my openness and friendliness may have been interpreted somehow as an invitation. Which, of course, it wasn't.

The worst aspect of the whole sorry saga was that I also made a decision at the time not to tell David anything about the incident. Once again, the decision was made when I was probably not thinking too clearly. I reasoned that being on the other side of the world he would feel totally helpless and impotent, therefore unable to support me or to handle the situation the way he would have liked (which no doubt would have involved calling the gendarmes). I also convinced myself, quite selfishly, that the attack would add to David's belief that I was not capable of looking after myself properly. That I was too open, that I exposed myself to risks and was therefore vulnerable to being preyed upon by men. So I said nothing when he phoned a few days later. I was now learning to lie, or at least to not admit to the truth, with some proficiency. It didn't feel good.

6

Since buying the village house, travelling back and forth between France and Australia has become the pattern of my life. I seem to spend increasing amounts of time hanging around airports and railway stations – the journey takes more than thirty-four hours each way, door to door. A plane from Bathurst to Sydney, then Sydney to Paris, usually with at least one stopover. Then a domestic plane from Paris to Toulouse, a bus from the airport to the railway station, and a train from Toulouse to Cahors, where I am met by either my friend Jock or by Jan and Philippe for the 45-minute car journey to Frayssinet. Then the same in reverse when I pack and return to Australia, to David and the farm. It takes me nearly a week to recover each time I do the trip, and every year I swear that I will do it only once each year. But somehow I seem to be commuting twice a year, often with an extra trip to India or Nepal if I have a trek organised.

My heart is in France yet my soul truly lies in Australia. Each time I return to Yetholme I am filled with a love for the farm and joy at being back in the bosom of my family. Although we have done very little to the appearance of the farmhouse, it always feels just right when I walk in the door, with the fires going and the family gathering for our customary happy and chaotic reunion. Our children and grandchildren love being at the farm, including Ethan and Lynne's little daughter Isabella, who has been diagnosed with a wide range of disabilities and who is lagging seriously behind her basic infant milestones. She lies on the floor kicking and giggling with the cats and dogs and older children all bouncing around her and keeping her well amused. It's a scene of familiar bliss.

It's been difficult for me to get a garden established at the farm, because since we first moved in I have been in France during the crucial planning and planting periods of autumn and spring. Although I can visualise how beautiful the place could look with just a bit of my passion for plants sprinkled around, I can't expect other people to look after a high-main-tenance garden when I am not there.

While I was in France, David established a business partnership with our son Ethan and a horticultural colleague from Ethan's workplace. Their plan is to build a native plant nursery at the farm, to supply bulk orders of trees and shrubs for roadside landscaping and bush regeneration projects. It's a great idea but it will take a lot of physical labour to get it up and running, not to mention cost as there are greenhouses to be built and expensive irrigation to be installed. The young men are totally enthusiastic and committed to the project and spend every weekend cleaning out sheds, building work spaces for the nursery and putting up the first enormous greenhouse. Although I also have lots of dreams of my own for the farm, I realise that these must be put on hold until the nursery is successfully established. I must also be realistic about my time and availability. I can't get a project up and running and then just disappear off to France for three months or more. Most aspects of farming take a long time to bear fruit and so I must wait until I can be assured of an uninterrupted run before getting anything started.

I have always loved keeping poultry, and one of my greatest delights at the farm is the large shed and run, which I quickly filled with chickens, ducks and geese when we first arrived. After decades of keeping chickens and ducks in a tiny space at Leura, the set-up at the farm seems like a luxury. As damage to the garden by scratching hens isn't an issue, I like to let the poultry free-range during the day, which I naturally prefer to keeping them penned. The sight of them grazing over the lawns and fossicking between the shrubs always fills my heart with joy.

But the young men have decided the poultry sheds are too close to the greenhouse and that there's a risk of rats damaging their plant stocks, because vermin are attracted to the grain stored for the birds. When I arrive home the fences of the run have been removed, the shed cleared and put to an alternative purpose, and a new shed and run erected much further from the house. The new shed, cobbled together from old bits of roofing iron, is far from satisfactory in my opinion, but I am assured improvements will be made. Within a few weeks, however, foxes raid the more vulnerable shelter and we lose all the chickens and most of the ducks.

In our first year at the farm we had a small herd of mixed cattle agisted in various paddocks around the farm, but again the boys believe they are counter-productive to the environ-mental management of the property. The cows blunder into the streams and precious wetland, polluting the water and eating back the reeds that bind the edges of the dams together. They also eat down all the tree seedlings that have been naturalising all over the farm, and so they must go. I love having animals around and would prefer that we fence off the sensitive areas and simply restrict the movement of the cows, but I am out-voted once again. The cows must go, and they do. Despite the drought, we are now faced with acres of long grasses, and the problems of snakes and bushfires concern me greatly. I agree that keeping animals can be damaging to the environment, but would prefer a compromise. I feel a sense of frustration but I also realise that the main focus of the farm is now the new nursery.

The drought itself is a huge worry to us and to all our farming neighbours. The stream – which, until thirty years ago, was a crystal-clear flow of water over a pebbly creek bed that was also home to families of playful platypus – is now a slimy, oil-slicked trickle. The roots of the crack willows, planted foolishly in the belief that they would bind together the banks of small streams, have choked the system, and the entire water table in our little valley appears to have dropped considerably. The spring which once fed our main dam has dried up and the dam level has dropped to within a metre of the muddy bottom. David finds a trout, a huge one, floating dead on the surface, its fleshy body bloated by the effects of the sun. Old-timers in the district say the stream has never been so dry, and there are rumours of springs drying up all around the neighbourhood.

So even if I did have the time and energy to start working on the garden, common sense tells me that I should leave it until the weather improves, until the dams are again filled with water and the stream has started flowing.

Despite our back-and-forth lifestyle, we have joined in with the community as best we can. A concerned neighbour phones us about a plan before the local council that would allow the new garage at the crest of the hill, on the main highway, to discharge its treated waste water into our fragile creek. It certainly is an issue that brings us all together, and we have several meetings and contact the media. David appears on the local news as a spokesperson for the group and passions run high. Given the drought and the problems with the local waterways already being polluted, we win the battle but the war will probably continue. It's all very disheartening, but this experience reminds us that although we live in a rural area, we are surrounded by wonderful neighbours.

7

My mother Muriel would have loved the farm here at Yetholme. It's several years now since she died and rarely does a day go by that I don't think of her. She lived with us for twenty-five years and our lives were intertwined, from the everyday mundane rituals to the special occasions of family life. She was there first thing in the morning, usually in rather a tetchy mood, desperate for her first cup of tea. Brewed in a pot with leaves – never teabags; white with one sugar. It's funny how these habits are passed down generationally. I drink my tea the same way, so do Miriam and Ethan, and of my eight grandchildren only one – Theo – likes a cup of tea. He drinks it the same way we all do.

Muriel was an unforgettable woman. In her youth she was arrestingly beautiful. Reed-thin, with milky skin, thick, wavy black hair and large blue-green eyes under arched black brows. A true Celtic rose. Her teeth were the only feature that let her down. A poor diet during the Depression and little understanding of dental hygiene meant that they were always weak and riddled with holes. After she married my father, the odd punch in the face didn't help. One of her front teeth was blackened in her twenties and by her late thirties, after three pregnancies, most of her teeth had fallen out. By the age I am now, mid-fifties, she had a full set of dentures.

Mum started smoking when she was seventeen and was still smoking heavily when she died at seventy-six. She was also an enthusiastic drinker and never let a day pass without a glass in her hand. She was, in my memory, a regular drinker who also maintained a certain discipline or set of rules around her imbibing. During the week, for example, she frowned on drinking during the day. When I developed a taste for French food and would cook us a little hot lunch, I would often pour myself a glass of wine to drink with it. This she considered shocking. Yet during the weekend it was open slather. Any time from eleven-thirty in the morning onwards was okay for a drink, followed by lunch then several more drinks and an afternoon nap.

Although she left school at fifteen, Mum was essentially an intellectual. She was a voracious reader, devouring the classics, especially Shakespeare who was her hero, and a broad spectrum of poetry which she could recite word-perfect. She loved fiction, classical and modern, and non-fiction, especially if it concerned politics. She was a long-time member of a book club and kept up with contemporary writing, and became the much-loved matriarch of her small group – most of them women in my age group. She was a communist and an atheist but also quite a spiritual woman. She believed she was fey as part of her Celtic heritage, which was totally at odds with her sceptical side. She was also incredibly superstitious. You could never put shoes on the table or open an umbrella in the house if my mother was around.

Although she never learnt to read music or play an instrument, Mum's knowledge of music was prodigious. As a young woman, in her first job as a secretary, she gave most of her wages to her widowed mother as board. The rest she spent on cigarettes and tickets to symphony concerts. She sewed her own clothes and made one pair of shoes last for a whole year so that she could indulge her passion for listening to music. She could identify virtually any piece of classical music on the radio from just a few bars, and was often also able to recognise the soloist or the conductor. She was passionate about music and my childhood was filled with the sounds of her passion. My brother and I didn't learn to read music, but all my children were proficient at this – mainly because their live-in grandmother constantly encouraged them. It was as though she invested the energy into her grandchildren that she hadn't been able to do with us because of our difficult family situation.

My mother was an outspoken, impatient, opinionated woman in an era when it was not considered appropriate for women to be assertive. She was capable of being utterly charming if it suited her, but more often than not it didn't. She didn't suffer fools gladly, and wasn't the slightest bit reluctant to let people know if they displeased or irritated her. As a child, I remember cringing in situations where my mother voiced her opinion in public. In the days before seatbelts, I recall throwing myself onto the floor of the car while my mother leant out the driver's window performing a rude gesture with her hand and shouting 'fuck you' at some hapless driver who had irritated her. Nineteen-fifties road rage. I remember a woman who queue-jumped at the local butcher shop being dressed down quite viciously by my mother – again I think I hid behind her skirts in embarrassment.

My mother's father was a journalist and also a drunk. Although quite a gentle and quiet man, he let his family down badly, especially my grandmother. So it always amazed me that my mother went on to marry a drunken journalist who was also not an ideal family man and who let her down very badly by womanising, spending most of his wages on his own indulgences, and occasionally hitting her in a domestic brawl. That said, people tend to re-enact their own family history – which is what puzzles me about myself at this stage of my life. I have made many conscious decisions to be different from my parents (and grandparents), but I am so much like them I find it impossible to escape.

My mother's career was chequered. She was forced to leave home before the Leaving Certificate because her father died and her mother needed her to work to help pay the rent. She did a short secretarial course and was quickly employed (ironically) by Penfolds Wines as a stenographer. At some stage, I'm not clear about when, she saw a job advertised as a 'copytaker' at the *Daily Telegraph* newspaper and applied. She was a crack shorthand writer and was given the job immediately.

This is where she met my father, who was at the time the News Editor. One of her first jobs was as a court reporter. Although she came from a well-read journalistic family herself, she had been, as most girls of that era were, quite sheltered. She told a funny story about a rape case she covered as a young and naïve court reporter. Part of the evidence submitted were sheets 'covered with semen'. Mum was a brilliant speller, but in this case she

typed 'seamen' and somehow must have carried the mental image of sailors sprawled all over the bed. My father took great delight in pointing out her innocence!

Mum was responsible for taking down in Pitman shorthand all the BBC broadcasts during the early part of the Second World War. There were no telexes or faxes or satellite links for news communications. Journalists in Australia had to stay up all night in the newsroom, tuned in to the BBC, and accurately transcribe speeches by Winston Churchill or whatever war news was being broadcast in London for the morning editions of the Sydney papers. Her accuracy was unfailing.

My mother fell hopelessly in love with my father, who was a widower with two young children. His first wife had suffered from depression and had been unable to cope with his difficult ways. She committed suicide, and for several years afterwards their children Jon and Margaret were cared for by a succession of family members and paid childminders. Having a beautiful young wife devoted to helping with the children must have been a wonderful relief for my father, who was quite ambitious and found it difficult to juggle work and his young family.

Immediately after their marriage, Dad was given a promotion and left for New York, where he had been assigned as foreign correspondent for the *Daily Telegraph*. It was difficult to get a place on a ship and Mum was left stranded in Sydney with her two young stepchildren for six months before joining Dad in his new job. It was certainly a good way for them to get to know each other, and they seemed to get along well from the start.

Jon remembers Muriel during this period as being fun-loving and elegant, always beautifully dressed and well groomed. Margaret, on the other hand, remembers the fights between

Mum and Dad much more vividly than anything else. Although there was rationing and shortages of various basic foodstuffs in America during the war, it appears there was no shortage of alcohol. It was in America that Mum developed her hard-drinking habits – partly, I suspect, through boredom because she didn't work at all during the four years they were overseas, and partly because Dad had a good income and spirits such as Scotch and bourbon were readily available and comparatively inexpensive. They lived in Manhattan for a while, then on Long Island, before finally moving out to New Canaan in Connecticut. Mum fell in with a hard-drinking crowd of wealthy locals and it seems that the war years were for her a constant round of socialising. Most of the photographs from that time show Mum looking gorgeous but often bleary-eyed, though she was only in her early twenties.

They remained in America until the end of 1947, then returned to Sydney. Curiously, my mother had never become pregnant during the early years of their marriage living overseas, but within a year of returning she did become pregnant and went on to have three children in rapid succession – my brother Dan, me, and my little sister Jane. This was the period of our family life that was the most traumatic. Although I have no memory of it, Mum drank heavily even during her pregnancies and when we were babies. This I was told by my sister Margaret when we finally met again in 2002. Mum's drinking, together with her constant fighting with my father, were two of the factors which prompted Margaret to escape on her eighteenth birthday and make her own way in the world.

Around this period, my baby sister Jane tragically died, my brother Jon became a marine engineer and left for the sea, and somehow Dan and I muddled along and survived.

Mum came to live with David and me when I was twenty-five and the mother of two young children, so essentially I only lived apart from her for about six years of my life. Dad had died and left her with very little financial security, so it seemed natural for her to become part of our growing young family. She was a great person to have around the house and everyone loved her, although there were times when her forceful personality made her difficult to live with. As she aged, her daily routine became fairly rigid. She developed a dislike of going out except once a week to the bank, the newsagency and the liquor shop – stocking up for the week ahead. She always woke early and had several cups of tea to revive her. She then read the newspaper from cover to cover and did the crossword and various word puzzles. Despite the haze of drinking and smoking, her mind remained sharp as a tack and she could take the ABC news down in shorthand until the day she died. She particularly loved finding fault in the work of other journalists, both in radio and print, and kept a notebook record of their grammatical or factual errors.

Although our children insist that Mum sometimes helped herself to the Scotch bottle during the day, I was only ever aware of her drinking in the evening. She would have an afternoon nap and then at five o'clock sharp she would march into the kitchen and grab two ice blocks from the freezer for her first drink of the day. Her consumption was fast and furious. The level on the Scotch bottle would drop dramatically between five and six p.m., and for me it was always a race to get a meal on the table before the seven o'clock news because by that time she would be utterly smashed. Like a lot of heavy drinkers, Mum lost interest in food and was gradually becoming thinner and more frail. She would fill up on alcohol before dinner, then just push the food around her plate. To try to overcome this, I changed her routine and started cooking her a hot lunch in the middle of the day, so that at least she would have something solid in her stomach before she hit the Scotch bottle at five.

If Mum was an outspoken woman when sober, she was totally uninhibited after a few drinks. Her penchant for saying exactly what she thought to anyone at any time caused me a huge amount of embarrassment when I was a child. But as I grew older and matured, I sneakily admired her forthrightness; although it could be alarming, it was mostly just very funny. When Miriam was first married, her husband Rick's family would come to visit and we liked them enormously. Once his elderly grandmother Phylis was visiting from England and she came for a family dinner which was a great success. Mum did her usual trick of drinking too much and disappearing off to bed without even saying goodnight. She reappeared an hour later, however, having obviously dozed off for a while. She was dressed in a ragged old nightie, her white hair was standing on end, and she had removed her teeth. She came over and sat beside Rick's grandmother and put her hand on her arm.

'You'll have to forgive me, Phylis,' she said to explain her earlier disappearance, 'but I'm pissed as a fucking newt.'

Spoken in her most cultured voice, it was a bit of a conversation stopper.

Mum no longer resembled the beautiful and elegantly dressed journalist she had once been, but the spirit of that young woman was always there. It never disappeared.

She often had falls in the evening although she rarely injured herself, which was amazing because I imagine her bone density must have been low. I organised for Home Help assistance to get her in and out of the shower as she grew more and more frail, and I also had handrails installed in the bathroom, toilet and hallways to try to minimise the number of accidents. Towards the end I bought her a commode chair – a handsome one make of oak that sat beside the bed so that she wouldn't have to brave the long hallway in the middle of the night to go to the toilet.

Mum's nightly ritual of drinking and going to bed early always culminated in a dramatic farewell. She had maintained her strong left-wing political beliefs and even though it had been decades since she was a member of the communist party she still admired much of what it stood for. Every evening she would emerge from her room to say a final goodnight, usually dressed for bed and looking rather raddled. Her parting words were invariably: 'Goodnight dear. I've got one last thing to say.' At which point she would raise her right arm in a defiant gesture. 'Up the revolution!' Then she would turn and disappear for the night.

Once a week Mum and I would meet friends at the pub in Wentworth Falls for a drink or two. One of them was the retired politician and judge Jim McClelland, who shared a left-wing political background with Muriel. It was one of the few occasions I could lure her out of her smoky bedroom. We would go to the pub at five o'clock and be back home by six-thirty to watch the ABC gardening show on which I was a presenter. It was an enjoyable ritual that got Mum out of the house for a while and into the company of others. She had steadily become a little reclusive and spent far too much time alone in spite of the fact that she was in the midst of such a large and busy family.

One rainy Friday she declined the weekly trip to the pub, saying she felt unwell. I tried to persuade her to come. 'You'll feel much better when we get there, Mum. Come on, it'll do you good to get out.' But she insisted on staying at home. I had barely arrived at the hotel when there was a phone message for me over the bar.

'Your son just called and asked if you could go home immediately. Apparently your mother is unwell.'

I was home in a flash. It was Ethan who had called. He had also called our GP, who had been with Muriel for several minutes before I got there.

'What's wrong with Grandma?' I asked Ethan.

'I don't really know,' he said, 'but she told me she had a pain in her abdomen. When I asked her what was wrong, all she said was, "I think I'm dying but don't tell your mother, she'll be worried."'

Our doctor, who was also a good family friend, said I must get Mum up to the hospital as quickly as possible. He was unable to make a firm diagnosis but could clearly see she needed immediate attention. He called an ambulance but there was none available. Apparently there had been a series of accidents on the highway as a result of the rain and we would have to wait two hours to get one.

'I'll take her myself,' I announced.

It's the funny things you remember in the midst of an emergency. There had been a delivery of cow manure for the garden that morning and the truck driver had dumped it outside the front gate. The rain had turned it into a soggy, smelly mess and somehow the doctor and I had to carry Mum over the cow manure to get to the car. The humour was not lost on her as we arrived in casualty stinking like a cow shed. There was a long queue but our doctor friend had phoned ahead to say that Mum must be given a bed to lie down on – she was too sick to sit on a chair in the outpatients waiting room.

What transpired over the next few hours is difficult to describe. The road accidents had filled the emergency room and there were not enough doctors to attend to the backlog of patients. Nobody had been seriously injured but there was a queue waiting to be seen, and Mum was quite a long way down the list. She was seen by a nurse, who was able to take notes but not offer any assistance in the way of pain relief. That would have to wait until a doctor could examine her. Mum's pain grew more and more intense. She was writhing on the narrow casualty bed and I tried my best to comfort her. It was appalling. I kept asking how much longer she would have to wait, but they kept saying they didn't know. At one stage I actually lay beside her on the bed, stroking her face and trying to soothe her. I was aware that none of the people being treated was critically or even seriously injured, but the hospital was handling cases in the order in which they had arrived. For four hours Mum was in agony, and eventually I couldn't deal with it any more and insisted loudly that a doctor must see her. *Now*. Not in ten minutes but *now*.

She was examined, but the young doctor on duty was uncertain about the cause of her pain. He ordered pain relief which worked almost instantaneously, much to my relief. She relaxed instantly once the terrible pain had been deadened.

'Mrs Moody,' the earnest young doctor said, 'I think we need to do some tests on you to find out what's causing the pain. I'm about to organise a Care Flight helicopter to pick you up and take you to Nepean Hospital.'

Mum had a flying phobia, which hadn't been an issue for a

while because she hadn't needed to fly anywhere for decades. 'Young man,' she said, again in her most cultured voice, 'I haven't flown for thirty years and I'm certainly not flying anywhere tonight.'

So an ambulance was ordered. I was advised to go home and get some sleep and then to drive down to Penrith in the morning to be with her for the tests. It's a decision I will always regret. I should have just gone with her in the ambulance, but somehow I thought she was going to be okay. She wasn't. She was dying as I kissed her goodbye and watched the ambulance head out of the hospital driveway and down the highway.

It was after midnight when I crawled into bed totally exhausted by Mum's painful ordeal. I thought it was a terrible state of affairs that an elderly woman, obviously in terrible pain, had been made to wait for four hours before being seen by a doctor. As I fell asleep I made a mental note to myself to write to the hospital and also to our local state member of parliament to complain about the inadequacies of the system.

I had not been asleep for long when the phone rang. It was Nepean Hospital. I must come immediately because my mother was gravely ill. David and I threw on our dirty clothes from the day before and drove like maniacs down the dark deserted highway. I knew she was dead and that they just hadn't wanted to say it over the phone. I repeated it over and over to David.

'She's dead, I know she's dead. I should have stayed with her. I should have gone with her in the ambulance.'

She was dead, of course, and they wheeled her into a small private area with curtains around so we could have some privacy. She had tubes going into her mouth and her face was distorted and strained. She did not look at peace.

I was totally stunned and barely able to speak. 'I need the children here now,' I said.

So David phoned them at their various homes and woke them from their sleep to get them to come to the hospital and sit with us. I had spoken to them all from the hospital earlier that evening to say that their Grandma was being admitted but that she seemed to be okay. So they all knew she was sick but none had expected this.

Miriam was pregnant with her second child. Little Eamonn was barely two and he played cheerfully around his great-grandmother's lifeless body, chomping on biscuits while the rest of us sat grimly trying to come to terms with what had just happened. We were shaken and in a weird state of disbelief. How could Grandma die? We all knew she was frail and that her health had been deteriorating for years now. But her character and her personality were so strong and so forceful that somehow none of us imagined that she could disappear. She seemed indestructible. Indomitable. Now here she was, a small grey shadow of a woman with tubes in her mouth. Muriel had gone.

8

The days between Mum's death and her funeral were a blur. I guess we were all in shock, but there was so much to be done. David was a great support, taking charge of so many of the practical things that needed organising and phoning people far and wide who needed to be told of Muriel's death. He chose the funeral directors because they were women and they wore white instead of the usual grim men in black suits. We had a fit of the giggles when they showed us the display booklet of 'caskets', all with their own special names. The Promethean was a gold-plated affair costing $40,000. We opted for the Essential, which was a plain wooden box for about $400. We had plans for it. In fact, we had plans for the entire funeral because we didn't want to just hand over the day to a funeral company. We wanted to be in control and make it our own. And Mum's, of course.

We placed a notice in death column of the *Sydney Morning Herald*. It was the usual wording, with one slight exception. Mum had been affectionately known as 'the old bag' since I was a child and we all called her that from time to time. Often her birthday cards were written to 'the old bag' rather than to Mum or Grandma. It was a family tradition and a term of endearment. So at the end of her death notice we simply said 'Farewell Old Bag'. It was picked up by the Column 8 editor, who made a disparaging remark about our disrespect for our 'deceased relative'. On any other occasion I would have written him a terse response, but there was too much going on at the time. Too much to be done.

We wanted to paint the coffin to personalise it. We wanted to bring Mum home for a night and have her lying in her coffin on the kitchen table. We all agreed that she had left in such a hurry that rainy Friday evening. She needed to come back and spend one last night at home with her family. We also wanted to have the funeral service at the house and not in a church or a crematorium. Mum hadn't been inside a church for decades and it seemed absurd to us to allow a stranger to conduct a funeral service. The women in white listened to all our requests and happily agreed. There was no reason why we couldn't do exactly what we wanted. Mum's body could be brought home and we could have the funeral around her in the kitchen where she had spent so many happy years.

Our son Aaron had just acquired his first car, a rather battered old white Kingswood ute, and he was charged with the task of picking up the empty casket from the western suburbs. On the way back up the mountains the engine overheated and he had to pull in to a service station for some water. An attendant came over to help him, took one look at the coffin in the back of the ute and fled. Aaron thought this was highly amusing.

We covered the kitchen table with newspapers and invited people to come and participate. I made a huge pot of Mum's favourite Irish stew and we filled the fridge with beer and wine. One by one friends came and each made a contribution to the decorating of the coffin. Aaron's closest friend from school, Jake, is a talented artist and he adored Muriel. He painted her portrait on the lid and perfectly captured her spirit. Another friend painted a cluster of yellow roses, Mum's favourite flowers, along the edge of the lid. Jenny Kee, known for her love of Australian flora, came by and painted a large bunch of bright red waratahs. We dipped little Eamonn's hands in red and blue paint and imprinted them along the side of the box. We tore pages from Mum's famous notebook – quotes and sayings from various journalists – and pasted them onto the wood.

As the evening wore on and we drank more wine, our inspiration escalated. Mum loved the chickens we kept in a coop in the back yard. I scooped them from their perches in the dark and they were subjected to having their feet dipped in paint. The side of the coffin became a colourful montage of chicken footprints, and there were also footprints on the back verandah where they walked after having been so rudely woken from their slumbers.

The following morning Aaron did the same trip in reverse, taking the garishly decorated casket back to the funeral parlour where Mum's body was lying. He took down her best outfit so she could be dressed, placed in the casket and brought back home for the last time. It was suggested by the ladies in white that they should bring her in the hearse rather than making the return journey in the back of Aaron's ute. They were probably right.

That last night we gathered again, eating, drinking and telling funny Muriel stories while she lay in state on the kitchen table. Most of the stories revolved around her capacity for outrageous behaviour. Aaron recalled only a month before when David and I were away for the weekend and he had decided to have a party at the house. Mum went to bed early as usual, then woke up and joined the party after midnight, dressed in her nightie. She sat up drinking with a gang of teenage boys for hours until she finally fell asleep on the sofa and they all carried her back to her bed. Typical. It felt good knowing she was there inside the box on the kitchen table with all these stories being told around her and about her. Everyone was laughing. Although we were terribly sad, we were also happy. Our memories of her were happy ones. It certainly helped.

The morning of the funeral, Miriam and I opened the coffin and applied a little make-up to Mum's face. We invited people for 11 a.m. and the plan was to leave for the cemetery at 1.30 p.m. We had organised champagne and lots of sandwiches. It was to be a party.

People gathered on the back lawn and drank champagne. David was the MC and we all spoke: David, Miriam, both my brothers, close friends and neighbours. My brother Jon reminded us what a beautiful and elegant young woman Muriel had been when he first knew her. Jim McClelland reminisced about their shared political beliefs. It was informal and sponta- neous and it all felt just right.

After the sandwiches, we opened the lid of the casket so that those who wanted to could see Muriel and say goodbye. Quite a few family and friends had said they didn't wish to see her in death, but somehow now they all did. They filed past her coffin and kissed her goodbye. There wasn't a dry eye in the house.

The hearse arrived and we hastily replaced the lid and the pallbearers marched her coffin around the garden she had loved so much, up and down the winding pathways and between the roses. She chose well to die in spring when the garden was at its peak. As they carried her out the front gate (I had removed the cow manure by this time), the entire party let out a thunderous cheer.

At the cemetery the mood was more sombre and sober. We placed her last half-empty bottle of Scotch and half-finished packet of cigarettes on the coffin as it was lowered gently into the ground. An Aboriginal friend told David that it is customary in their culture for the deceased to be associated with a favourite animal or bird which is symbolic at the moment of interment. Mum had always loved the noisy currawongs that came up from the valley every autumn and sheltered in our garden. So we called out 'currawong, currawong' as a parting gesture. When we looked up into the gum trees at the back of the cemetery there were currawongs everywhere, watching.

Mum was a Celt and fiercely proud of her heritage. We built a traditional cairn of stones over her grave. She also loved the symbolism of the Celtic cross and we had one made for her from sandstone with her name, Muriel Flora Moody, and date of birth and death inscribed. Under her name we have carved the words 'Up the Revolution'.

9

Our seventh grandchild, Isabella Rosa, with her Italian ancestry on her mother's side and her sweep of burnished red hair from her Celtic side, has all sorts of medical problems. She was conceived by our youngest son Ethan and his partner Lynne on the eve of their departure for France on an extended working holiday. The only hitch was that they had no idea Lynne was pregnant as they set off with the expectation of exploring Europe in between stretches of working wherever they could find employment, as well as doing some basic renovation to our little village house.

Lynne felt ill from the day they first set foot on French soil and after six weeks of blaming her symptoms on jetlag, a virus and even the local water, she tentatively bought a home pregnancy testing kit at the local pharmacy. The result was positive.

It was not a good pregnancy because Lynne was either vomiting or felt nauseous for most of it. She gained weight, but not nearly as much as the local midwife she consulted every four weeks would have liked. The French medical system is very thorough and she underwent all the routine tests. One of them, taken in her fifteenth week, indicated that she was in the 'medium to high risk' category for a baby with a chromosomal disorder. An amniocentesis was recommended but given their age (both in their early twenties) and positive attitude towards the pregnancy, they decided to decline. In any event, even if a complication was confirmed, it would be too traumatic to do anything about it this far into the pregnancy. So they waited it out with great optimism.

At seven months, they cut short their European adventure, after bravely exploring regions of Holland, France and Spain despite Lynne's permanently queasy stomach, and returned to Australia to prepare for the birth.

Ethan and Lynne have always been a very mature couple despite their tender years. They have been together since they were seventeen and travelled north to the Lismore region to undertake their tertiary studies at an age when most young people are still living at home, expecting their Mum to cook their dinner and do their washing.

Indeed I used to worry about their sober and responsible attitude to life, thinking they had grown old well before their time without ever having been outrageous, irresponsible kids. One chilly winter evening when they were first living together I called around to see them and was startled to find them cuddled up knitting a blanket – out of cast-off scraps of wool they had been given by Lynne's Sicilian grandmother – Lynne at one end, Ethan at the other. I went home and said to David, 'I'm really worried about those two. They're like an old married couple. They should be out having fun, not sitting at home knitting. They're more settled than we are.'

Or ever have been, I probably should have added.

They were always good at managing money and saving. From the beginning, our family nickname for Lynne has been 'budget woman' for her uncanny ability to save even on a student income. Unlike our other children who, from time to time in their student years, got into financial scrapes and called out for some urgent parental assistance, Ethan and Lynne have always managed brilliantly under their own steam. It was this resourcefulness that enabled them to save enough to fly to France and to travel as much as they did during their foreshortened stay in spite of the fact that Lynne had been too unwell to work after they arrived.

Now, of course, we are thankful for their maturity and their ability to cope with whatever life throws at them. For they have accepted not only that their first-born is profoundly disabled, but that she will probably require their care and devotion for the rest of her life.

There isn't a definitive diagnosis for what ails Isabella, although the pointers are towards some sort of rare chromosomal disorder compounded by a multitude of problems that may or may not be associated. She was tiny when she was born in January 2002. Only 2050 grams, or 4 pounds 10 ounces. The birth went quite smoothly, with our daughter Miriam by Lynne's side as her 'labour supporter'. It's one of the things I treasure about my large and affectionate family. Our children are all there for each other and there is a continuity in their relationships which often revolves around the joyous occasion of birth. When Ethan was born in the front room at Leura, Miriam was by my side the entire time, mopping my brow with a wet washer and watching in awe the long and often arduous process of birth. After me, Miriam was the first person to hold Ethan and they bonded like glue from that first moment. They still adore each other.

When Miriam had her first son, a homebirth, while she was a final year university student in Canberra, Ethan insisted on taking time off school to come to the birth. She desperately wanted him to be there. He was only fourteen and the midwife said afterwards that he was the most 'together' young man she had ever seen helping at a birth. He came to the birth of Miriam's next two sons and was sadly disappointed that he and Lynne were in France when her fourth baby boy was born in Bathurst.

Now here they were together again, this time for the birth of Ethan's first child.

Lynne laboured well until it was almost time for the second pushing stage of labour. She was connected to a CTG machine which suddenly indicated that the baby was becoming distressed. It was decided to prepare Lynne for a caesarean section and while the midwifery staff were getting organised Lynne, being comforted by a very frightened Ethan and Miriam, suddenly felt an overwhelming urge to push. With a little encouragement from Miriam, she did just that and within minutes Isabella was born, tiny but to all intents and purposes perfect. Indeed, the paediatrician on duty pronounced her 'perfectly formed and quite normal' in spite of her diminutive size. However, Miriam was concerned even then that something was not quite right. The placenta, when delivered, was also very small. It appeared as though Isabella had not been nourished adequately during the pregnancy. Something was amiss.

Lynne was a devoted mother from day one. She had been told to 'feed and feed' Isabella to try and compensate for her low birth weight. Night and day, every hour, she put that tiny baby to the breast and although Isabella didn't have a strong sucking reflex she tugged at the nipple sufficiently for the milk supply to let down and trickle down her throat. She gained weight, slowly but steadily, and became more responsive as the weeks went by. But not nearly as responsive as she should have been.

When I saw Isabella during those early months she was always contented. Sweet-natured and not at all demanding. Her red hair formed a bright halo around her circular beaming face and she seemed like a delicate little doll rather than a robust newborn baby. She didn't cry but made strange mewing sounds and as she grew she started growling. We nicknamed her 'tigerbaby'.

The first indications of a problem were muscular. She just didn't seem to be using her arms and legs or holding her head up strongly like a normal baby. She was floppy and made no effort to support her weight when held up with her feet on your lap. Within the family, we started to be concerned but decided that discovering if there were problems with their daughter was a journey that Ethan and Lynne must make in their own time – that there was no purpose in us nagging them about her slow development when surely the community nurses and the paediatrician overseeing her would quickly detect that things were not progressing as they should. But it was not to be a quick response.

Part of the problem was, I am sure, that it would take Ethan and Lynne quite a while to acknowledge that Isabella had permanent disabilities. For a long time they clung to the idea that her 'delayed development' was the result of her low birth weight and that she would somehow miraculously catch up with her peers, the same way premature babies do over a period of some years. Gradually, however, it became obvious to all of us that Isabella was very different. Unique, in fact. From six months onwards her differences were acknowledged and totally accepted by her young parents and the search was on for answers, a diagnosis. The never-ending testing had begun.

The first and most crucial problem to solve was Isabella's inability to feed properly. For six months her diet had been the best food for all newborn babies – breast milk – but now she was failing to thrive, starting to go backwards. Lynne tried patiently for weeks and weeks to introduce solid foods but Isabella seemed incapable of swallowing. She rolled the food around her mouth and pushed it out. She gagged if forced. To try and boost her growth, a nasogastric tube was inserted into her nostril, although Lynne also continued to breastfeed. I went to the hospital on the day they were to insert the tube for the first time. I wanted to be supportive. Ethan and Lynne held tiny Isabella as still as possible on the examination table while the nurse pushed the tube down her tiny oesophagus. I held down her protesting little feet. Ethan and Lynne were calm despite the traumatic nature of the procedure and I was a quivering wreck, tears cascading down my cheeks at the distress of our tiny baby. If I had known then what Isabella would endure over the next two years, I would have been even more distraught.

Isabella's muscles have never worked properly, inside or outside. Her digestive system doesn't function efficiently. Her bowels are also sluggish and require constant suppositories and enemas to keep them functioning. She requires feeding around the clock – after twelve months the nasal tube was replaced by a stoma, which means her formula is delivered directly into her stomach in small doses every hour or so. She can only tolerate the simplest formula and even on that regime her body regularly becomes overloaded and protests by rejecting the food. Some-times she vomits solidly for days at a time.

She requires physiotherapy on a daily basis. Until she was two years old her disabilities were not properly recognised, because there was no definitive diagnosis. Without a 'name' to pin to a disability, it's difficult to get financial support from the wide range of services within the community health system. Now, thankfully, the entire local medical profession has swung behind the young couple and Isabella is under the constant care of a dietician, a physiotherapist, a speech pathologist, an occupational therapist, as well as myriad paediatricians with specialities that range from neurological to gastro-enterological. Ethan and Lynne are entitled to home help for several hours a week and assistance to take Isabella for regular hydrotherapy at a heated indoor pool. Isabella also attends a regular day care centre twice a week and has her own carer who manages her complicated feeding regime and provides the much-needed stimulation.

As if Isabella's problems were not enough, she has also been diagnosed now as being deaf – up to 90 per cent total hearing loss. And vision-impaired.

As with all tragedies, there are positives. First and foremost is Ethan and Lynne's unflinching ability to cope with every aspect of Isabella's care. Not only have they totally accepted her condition, they have embraced it. Instead of wallowing in self-pity and asking themselves 'How could this happen to us?' or 'Why our baby?' they have claimed their daughter as the most special and delightful of all children. They dote on her and lavish her with attention and concern for her development. They make caring for Isabella look easy when we all know it is far from that. The sleepless nights, the constant demands, the worry when her bowels decide to stop working and she slips into pain and distress. The knowledge that she may never walk and talk like other children, that she will never reach her genetic potential. They take it in their stride like the mature young couple they have always been. Perhaps they were that way for a reason.

The other positive is Isabella herself. Despite her myriad disabilities, she is the most engaging little person. Smiling widely, she now has a full complement of teeth and she waves her hands in excitement when you catch her eye or make physical contact. She is enormously responsive to human interaction and everyone in her orbit is drawn to her. In a way, her whole being is charismatic and wherever she goes you will find people leaning over her pram and talking to her, or stroking her face. It's impossible to come into a room where Isabella is and not want to make contact with her. She is totally irresistible. When the family gathers, Isabella is put in the centre of the family room floor, usually hooked up to her feeding tube and surrounded by bright, tactile toys. Within minutes the other children join her on her purple rug, lying with their faces on the floor talking to her. Nobody tells them to, they just do it.

Lynne and Ethan have also sought the advice of alternative medical practitioners to help with Isabella, especially with her ongoing feeding problems. She has been seen by naturopaths and more recently a local herbalist who uses iridology (examination of the eyes) to aid in diagnosis. Lynne made an appointment with Kaye without realising that I had consulted her myself, nearly twenty-five years ago, with Ethan when he was a baby. Ethan was a fussy feeder and during his first six months he was often unsettled and colicky. Kaye's treatment helped enormously. Under her guidance I modified my diet and she also prescribed Bach flower remedies to calm Ethan down. It worked. Having not seen Kaye for years, we met accidentally in Leura one day.

'I've just met your granddaughter Isabella,' were her first words to me.

'Isn't she beautiful,' I replied with pride.

'She's an amazing child,' Kaye replied. 'I looked into her eyes and couldn't believe what I saw. There's a lot going on in there. Much more than any of us realise. She's a very special little person.'

Kaye was confirming what we instinctively knew to be the truth. Isabella has come into our family as the most precious gift of all. She is like a shining light and will always, always be surrounded by love.

10

During the period in late 2002 when I was wrestling with the writing of *Last Tango* there was something important I neglected to tell David. Neglected isn't the right word. It was something else, like the sexual attack in the village house, that I had deliberately decided not to tell him. Keeping such important information to myself naturally created a vast schism between us.

When I fell in love with the man from Toulouse, David sensed it immediately. Even before it was a reality – when it was little more than a long-distance email and phone infatuation – he picked up on my signals and observed my moods and behaviour to confirm in his own mind that troubled times were ahead. After the affair ended we spent weeks and months in painful discussion, agonising about the rift in our relationship. Once trust has been betrayed it is almost impossible to regain. David admitted that one of the main problems, from his perspective, was the probability that my infidelity would lead to further affairs. That I wouldn't stop at one.

At the time I railed against this notion. The affair had happened only because I had fallen in love. It wasn't a shallow sexual adventure, it was a deeply heartfelt relationship that had been difficult to sever and extremely painful, not only for David but also for me and the man involved.

But it wasn't that simple. That I had fallen in love was certainly the truth, but the affair had also triggered in me a sexual charge that I found difficult to ignore. The fact that David and I had always enjoyed a full and satisfying sex life didn't seem to make any difference. I was experiencing mid-life sexual curiosity and I couldn't switch it off or bury it. It was now part of me and it meant that I looked at the world and at myself through different eyes. The 'me' that I had felt so confident in and secure with for the past thirty years had somehow vanished and been replaced by a new and different me. A more sexually overt me. Perhaps it was because I had been in the same monogamous relationship since I was twenty-one, and that before falling in love and getting together with David I had been relatively inexperienced. I had never really sown my wild oats and now, I feared, time was running out.

The change in me was patently obvious. I shed a lot of weight and started exercising to improve my muscle tone. I changed my hairstyle and the way I dressed. While these physical manifestations didn't happen overnight, they were clearly obvious to my friends and family. It wasn't consciously calculated. I didn't sit down and formulate a makeover plan for myself, a blueprint for how I wanted to look. I simply became much more aware of my appearance, and I expect this is why I started worrying about lines and wrinkles and other external signs of ageing. None of these superficial concerns had ever been an issue for me until now and, while intellectually I could see what was happening, I didn't have the ability or the desire to prevent the changes from happening. It was too exciting.

It was an eventful year. In January, Ethan and Lynne gave birth to Isabella Rosa. In May, I went to France and the UK to lead a garden tour and I started my clandestine relationship with the man from Toulouse. At the end of May, David joined me for several weeks holiday following the Cannes Film Festival. He went back to Australia, leaving me to work on the book. I continued the affair, totally swept away by the excitement of it. David then confronted me the moment I arrived back home in Australia in late July. In September, I was back in France on my own, ostensibly to continue working on the book but also to lead the first of the regional village walking tours I had planned the year before. While obviously not all that thrilled that I was in France without him, given what had just happened, David somehow trusted me enough to believe that I was working hard. Which I certainly was.

The problem is that when in France I feel energised in a way that I haven't felt for years. I socialise much more intensively, burning the candle at both ends night after night. In Australia, I concentrate on my immediate family and a small but much-loved group of friends. In France, I have a wide and varied coterie of new friends and acquaintances, and even though by September the busy summer season has finished, the social life is constant and stimulating. Naturally, there are a lot of men around – both married and unmarried – and I enjoy their reaction to the new me. Being an Australian is also a bit of a novelty in this region. Australian women tend to be more open and expressive than their English or French counterparts; less hidebound by culture, tradition or class, and often more garrulous. I revel in the company of my lively friends, especially when gathered around a table of good food and wine. I tell the most outrageous jokes and enjoy the shocked reaction that comes from risqué tales being told by a woman.

Among my large and varied circle of friends is a man I have known since I first came to this region in 2000. Intelligent, articulate and single. Our paths cross socially from time to time although he lives quite a distance from our village. I always found him attractive and interesting, but I had never contemplated a sexual relationship with him. Nearly ten years younger than me, he has been living alone for three years, having separated from and then finally broken up with his long-standing French girl-friend. His work takes him overseas several times a year, so he isn't always around at the same time as I am. This eventful year, however, he's around constantly and, knowing he lives alone, I invite him over for dinner several times. On the surface it's all quite harmless.

He's quite a reserved person and although our conversations bounce energetically around all manner of topics, from politics to poetry and music, from religion and ethics to sex, he is quite reticent on a personal level. Intellectually he's out there, but emotionally it's as though he has a protective wall built around himself. I find it quite appealing and ponder if there is a way of breaking down the wall. Discovering what's on the other side.

One evening after a dinner at my house followed by several hours of animated conversation, he suddenly realises how late it is and gets up to leave. The residual mess from our meal is scattered on the table and kitchen bench and I'm feeling rather woozy from all those hours of drinking wine. As he bends to give me the customary polite farewell kiss on each cheek, I put my arms around his neck and kiss him squarely on the mouth. I hadn't been sitting there thinking about it while we were talking – I would have been a nervous wreck if I'd been anticipating and planning such a bold attempt at seduction. It's a spontaneous impulse. Unpremeditated, impetuous and completely reckless. Instead of drawing away from me, he steps forward and puts his arms around me, our bodies touching for the first time. I feel a rush of warmth and retreat, drawing a few deep breaths to steady myself.

'I think I'd better go home,' he says.

'Yes, you should,' I reply, probably too quickly.

Without turning back, he walks out into the cool of the evening and heads straight for his car. I close the door immediately without standing and waving him off as I would normally do.

What *was* that? I think to myself. You must be mad. You really are losing your marbles. Without clearing up the dinner debris, I retreat to my bed but lie awake for what seems like hours, trying to process the events of the evening. Trying to make sense of my actions and his response to them. But I can't make sense of it. It is all totally beyond me.

11

 Given the lateness of the previous night's events and my trepidation about talking to the man I had kissed so clumsily, I hesitate until well after nine the next morning before telephoning him. He sounds bright and chirpy when he answers the phone and I launch immediately into a babble of apologies and explanation.

'I'm really sorry about last night. I don't know what was wrong with me. I must have had too much to drink. I'm very emotional at the moment. So I'm sorry, really sorry.'

There's a long pause. I sense a nervous laugh.

'Don't be sorry,' he said. 'I enjoyed it. Nothing quite as nice as that has happened to me for a long time.'

Another long silence as I catch my breath.

So it began.

It's impossible to describe the machinations of the mind in such a situation. Mine is totally overloaded with wild thoughts and mad ideas buzzing around at a thousand miles an hour. It's difficult to be still for a moment and certainly almost impossible to sleep. I feel as though I am playing a frantic game of football inside my head, dashing from one end of the field to another, dodging and weaving. Feeling high one moment and low the next. Elation and excitement churned up with fear and a total sense of disbelief.

There is no place or space for logic or calm consideration. I am compelled, all the while knowing that the consequences of my actions may very well be disastrous. It's a very dangerous game and I have so much to lose: my family, the farm, the life I have created over the last thirty-two years and, most importantly, my still-powerful, if often tumultuous, relationship with David.

Once again I experience the all-too-familiar sensation of suspension of reality. Is this happening to someone else? It isn't me at all. I don't do this sort of thing. Is it a just game? It feels like it is. I am leading a double life. At home in Australia is the real world. The family, the farm, my work, my children, my grand-children and David. Here in France I am living a fantasy. The village, the little stone house, the markets, the restaurants, the wine and the lovers. It is all too wonderful and terrifying to be true. I have it all. My senses are so alive I feel I could burst out of my skin.

We see each other virtually every day and endeavour to be discreet. He doesn't feel comfortable coming to the village house so most nights, very late, we end up back at his place. We don't talk very much about what we are doing, we simply allow it to carry us along. Having broken through the barriers he has built around himself, I find my new lover to be quite a surprise. A delightful surprise. When we are alone together he is a different person. Passionate, uninhibited and very giving. He has let his guard down and allowed me into a secret place in his life. He explains that it takes him a long time to feel totally comfortable with a woman, to feel secure enough to be himself. He's been hurt in the past and is determined, I suspect, never to be hurt that way again. In many ways he brings out the nurturing side of me. He has a certain vulnerability that makes me want to look after him. Mother him. It's a common attraction for women and is not simply because I am several years older than him. Once or twice I ask him how he is feeling. What his thoughts are about our relationship. He is, as I probably should have expected, reticent and non-committal. All he will say is that he is 'pleased' that our relationship has moved onto a different level. That it is a lot of fun. It certainly is. But the seriousness of what we are doing is hovering, always in the background.

Whatever happens, David must never find out this time. It would be the end. More than he could tolerate. He has already suffered enough, I simply have to keep my cool and not allow my emotions to give the game away. I must learn to lie, something I have never been very good at. When he phones from Australia I do my best to sound carefree and bright, filling him in on the business of my days, the plans I am making for renovating the house, the feedback from the walking tour, which has been a great success.

How am I feeling through all this? Well, after the initial shock of it wears off and I reconcile myself to the fact that it is real, that it is actually happening to me, I feel a thrilling sense of abandonment. Having a younger lover is exciting and I relish the wickedness of it. I enjoy being a 'bad girl' and, even though I know it is completely without moral justification, I love every moment of it. It is like a drug and I am addicted.

I try not to ponder the rights and wrongs of the situation, I just want to experience every sensation to the full and I use my all-too-familiar life-coping strategy of burying my head in the sand in order to avoid confronting what is happening in my life. I have always had the ability to put difficult issues in the 'too hard basket' to avoid thinking about them and therefore to avoid having to deal with them. It is the same mechanism I used as a child to deal with the painful circumstances of my dysfunctional and disruptive family life. It is the same technique I employed during my long relationship with David as a way of avoiding those aspects of our life together that I found frustrating or deeply unsatisfying. Indeed, I now realise that for most of my adult life I have crowded my days with busyness and demands both on a professional and personal level as a way of side-stepping various truths that I don't wish to confront. I am certain a lot of people do exactly the same thing – evading the deeper issues of life by just being far too busy and involved to stop, take stock and make difficult decisions.

This time I am determined not to get caught up in the emotional side of the relationship. I certainly feel love for this man and a strong attachment to him because of our friendship over the past three years, but I don't wish to experience the pain of the last affair. I don't want to fall head over heels in love – this must be more cut and dried. Obviously there is closeness brought about by intimacy, yet there is also a sense of detach-ment – as though we both know it must not be a permanent arrangement but a delicious interlude in our lives. Without obli-gation or commitment and certainly without responsibility. Not that there is anything casual or flippant about the relationship. It is intense and there is undeniable electricity between us when we find ourselves thrown together by social circumstances.

I suspect this is why love affairs are so compelling. A lot of men, my father included, spend their entire married lives conducting a series of extra-marital sexual relationships – not because they don't love their wives, but because there is a powerful thrill in illicit relationships. The first signals of attraction; the body language and chemistry; the first touch – which may be little more than an accidental brushing of skin against skin; the first kiss; the inevitable seduction.

It's what happens as the relationship evolves that is important. Is it to be an affair that changes the course of your life? Ends a marriage or even two marriages? Breaks up families and causes widespread pain or disruption? Or should it remain a secret between the lovers? A shared intimacy that brings pleasure and joy to the couple without hurting anyone else?

The danger is, of course, not simply in being discovered. It is the risk of falling in love and therefore becoming so overwhelmed by and attached to the new relationship that it seems impossible to let it go. That's exactly what happened to me last time, and I was forced to make the ultimate choice between my husband and family and my lover. This time I am determined not to fall in love – and certainly not to be discovered.

12

 For me, life in Frayssinet has always been a hive of social activity. It is here that I burn the candle at both ends. My life in Australia has always had a strong element of socialising, but over the past decade the shift has been from friends and work colleagues to my own ever-expanding family. I simply don't have the energy to cook for and entertain friends when the weekends are often taken up with large family gatherings that involve the preparation of mountains of food and all the accompanying caring for and clearing up after small children.

So France has become a very special place for me, because it is where I enjoy the company of friends almost to the exclusion of all else. While I get homesick and certainly do miss the little ones, I also revel in the freedom of being able to spend time with friends whenever and wherever I please. I haven't really been able to do that since before I had children and I am sure most working mothers would recognise the situation – family and work commitments always seem to take priority over just plain 'having fun'.

David finds the social life in France overwhelming. He's much more of a homebody and can't keep up with the pace of the life I lead when I am 'in residence' in the village. There's always something happening and I seem to be out virtually every night in the summer and often busy during the day as well – either meeting my mix of expat and French friends for drinks or a visit to markets or having a 'serious' lunch. Lunch *is* serious in France, and I can't resist being part of the spirit of it all.

My friends are diverse. Many are funny and odd, even eccentric, and while they don't all get along with each other, we somehow muddle along amid frequent social gaffes and the occasional outright embarrassment. There's an undercurrent to social life here that I have only really begun to discover by coming back year after year. During my first visit I viewed the social scene through rose-coloured glasses, but now the more subtle nuances of the life here are beginning to sink in. I try to ignore them as much as possible, but it isn't always possible.

My good mate Jock is somehow at the centre of my social scene because everyone seems to love him and to realise that a lunch or dinner with Jock will never be boring. He speaks very softly, which can be a problem at large, noisy gatherings, and he often remains subdued early in the evening, so that those who don't know him may be fooled into thinking he is shy. But Jock is crafty. He's simply biding his time. Getting a feeling for the room and the other guests. He usually starts with the odd one-liner. A quip that is perfect for whatever is being discussed. Then come the jokes – every year he seems to acquire a new repertoire. And finally, as the evening begins to disintegrate with too much good food and wine, Jock starts with anecdotes of his years as a journalist – first in New Zealand, then Australia and finally in

New York. They are mostly hilarious, often self-deprecating, and demonstrate his wit and the path he trod to develop his easygoing philosophy of life. He sometimes falls off his chair with enthusiasm as the anecdotes get more lively, and our friend Roger, the English artist, describes this as 'Jock's attention-getting behaviour'. Roger has drawn the most delightful action cartoon of Jock in the process of falling backwards off his plastic chair.

Roger too is a larger-than-life character. He lives half the year in a small cottage on the outskirts of a remote village and the other half at Brighton in the UK, where he is surrounded by a vibrant artistic and cultural scene. The best of both worlds. Last summer Roger and his wife Ann installed an in-ground pool at their French cottage and the ongoing saga of its construction, with the accompanying fiascos and communication breakdowns with the tradesmen, kept us entertained all summer long. It was finished just in time for the autumn cool. It's hard to lure Roger out of his studio and garden – he's become a bit reclusive these last few years – but when he can be inveigled into an outing it's always a bonus. He throws outrageous parties – often fancy dress – and prefers inviting people to dinner to being asked out.

Jan and Philippe remain constant companions, although they have become more subdued these past few summers. Jan, like Jock, was born in New Zealand but has spent most of her life in the northern hemisphere. She gave up alcohol a few years back and now drinks a variety of 'mock' champagnes while we quaff the wonderful local reds. It must sometimes be alarming for her to observe the conversation and general demeanour of the table deteriorating as the night wears on. Philippe is a landscaper, so they are therefore rarely available for lunch – and if they do come to dinner they tend to flag early. The big difference is that while so many of the people in our circle are retired and can sleep off the excesses of the night before the following morning, poor Jan and Philippe are usually up at dawn to start work. They find the late nights totally exhausting. Jan is also very careful about her weight and eats like a bird, which seems madness when, like all of us, she is constantly surrounded by so much tempting food and wine. She stoically endeavours to keep Philippe on a punishing 'health regime', but every so often he breaks out and falls ravenously upon the foie gras and the red wine. It's good to see. Jan is my translator and support system for the walking tours and we always have a riotous time together – feeding, entertaining and guiding our Australian visitors around this corner of the world that we both love so much.

Philippe, like most of my French friends, is fascinated by all things Australian. The French, on the whole, don't travel overseas as often as many other nationalities, but they certainly read a lot and watch documentaries about foreign countries, and Australia is always one of their favourites. I have a lot of fun teaching Philippe slang expressions, which he trots out at social gatherings to the amusement and amazement of everyone. I taught him to say, when feeling thirsty, that he is 'dry as a dead dingo's donga', which he pronounces with such an alarming accent on the word 'donga' that people fall off their chairs with laughter. Someone else then taught him to say, 'I am so hungry I could bite the crotch out of a low flying duck', which is totally appropriate given the quantity of duck eaten in our region. Finally, I taught him the expression, 'Don't come the raw prawn with me', which he just adores but gets wrong every time because of the order in which the French language places words.

'Hey Mary,' he says with gusto, 'don't come on me with your raw prawn.' It brings the house down.

I also teach Christian and Christiane from the bar to say 'gidday' as a greeting, and they use it regularly instead of 'bonjour'. It results in very strange expressions on the faces of their French customers, and once again their pronunciation is way off the mark. It makes me feel a little better about my muddled French!

Claude, the retired photographer, has recently undergone heart surgery but it doesn't seem to have slowed him down. Being from England, he could have had his operation in London using a top surgeon, but chose instead to go to a hospital in Toulouse that has the reputation of being the best facility for heart surgery in the world. While the operation and immediate aftermath were traumatic, Claude has bounced back in his inimitable style. He exercises daily and watches his food and alcohol consumption to some degree, which results in his looking at least a decade younger than his chronological age. He still loves to tap on my window just as the church bells chime at midday, in the hope I might join him for 'une verre' at the bar. Invariably we end up lunching together, often with a few other waifs and strays who have wandered into the bar at lunchtime.

Claude's only concession to ageing is his vagueness, which appears to have plateaued but is nevertheless quite noticeable to his friends. I suspect he has always been a bit vague; it's just that it's become more apparent of late. His way of dealing with the problem is to write himself reminders on yellow Post-it notes which he sticks in obvious places so he will be reminded of what he needs to do. On his bedside phone will be the note he'll see on waking, reminding him of his first few chores of the day. By the main phone are numerous notes with instructions about which tradesmen he needs to call and what myriad small jobs require attending to around his large house and garden. On the back door he leaves notes about what he needs to do when he goes out shopping – these are quite apart from the actual shopping list. His house seems perpetually covered in yellow sticky notes, and even then he still manages to forget things. In preparation for a trip to the UK, he bought hundreds of euros' worth of glorious French cheeses and some local saucisson to distribute among his English friends and family. Despite a note on the back door reminding him to pack the tasty gifts into an esky and put it in the boot of the car, he left the lot behind and we were the beneficiaries, after a frantic phone call.

'For heaven's sake, help yourselves to the cheeses in the fridge,' he bleated on his mobile phone from the English Channel ferry terminal. 'They'll be off by the time I get back.'

Indeed, Claude's generosity can sometimes cause a problem, because people tend to take advantage of his 'open house' policy. When he goes away, he often leaves the keys to the house with friends in the hope they'll keep an eye on things, and he then invites them to 'have a dinner party' and 'help yourselves to the wine in the fridge'. Which we have all done on occasions when he's been away travelling.

One year he left me the keys because I was clearing his phone answering machine and feeding the ducks that live on the millstream that runs under his house. As Claude's dining room is so large, I did have a party, inviting several of the locals. It was to be a progressive dinner. Miles and Anne, who come down from London to their house just outside the village several times a year, were in town and, as Miles had recently been to a conference in Moscow, he invited a group of us for 'vodka and caviar' as a first course. The plan was for the dinner party – which also included Jock, Jan and Philippe and Anthony from the next village – to then move down to Claude's for pizza, salad, cheese and dessert. All went to plan, except that the vodka was much stronger than most of us expected (Miles knew, but didn't really let on). So spirits were high by the time we reached Claude's, and even higher by the time we drank our supply of wine and ate the pizzas. Jan and Philippe left straight after dinner, because of their usual early start the following day.

Remembering Claude's parting words – 'Help yourselves to the wine' – I said that I was sure he wouldn't mind if we had a couple of bottles, thinking I could probably easily replace them the following day. Miles had other ideas. He knew that, quite apart from the wine in the kitchen, Claude also had a well-stocked cellar, and he suspected there were some bottles 'about to go off'. I am ashamed to say that, despite a few vigorous protestations (from Anne) we drank a bottle of very, very good vintage wine with all sorts of ludicrous justifications being bandied about: 'We're really doing Claude a favour'; 'This wine would have gone off in another six months'; 'It's a shame to let good wine like this go to waste'.

Outrageous. I felt honour-bound to confess our misdeeds to Claude when he returned. He was not at all amused, and the aftermath caused quite a ripple for the entire summer. Being the holder of the key, I felt responsible for the episode and we had a whipround and bought Claude several bottles of good quaffing red. But nothing that could match his now totally unavailable Mouton Rothschild.

Whoops.

13

When David's mother Mary turned ninety we flew to her home city of Wellington in New Zealand to join her celebrations. She's an amazing woman – a combination of intelligence and strength of character, mingled with a certain fragility. She threw her own party in the quaint but rather stuffy clubhouse of the golf club where she still plays at least two rounds of nine holes a week. Despite long-term eye problems, Mary has a current driver's licence, is an avid fan of live theatre, movies and concerts, walks vigorously around the bay in the wildest and windiest of weather and swims at the nearby harbour beach many months of the year. Until last year she travelled overseas regularly, even tackling walking tours in Italy and Greece well into her eighties. She is formidable.

At her birthday lunch she took to the microphone and gave a stirring speech, stating emphatically that growing old 'isn't for sissies'. Although she has an older brother and one younger sister, Mary has lost her husband, a sister and many of her friends and neighbours to old age. While she hasn't stopped living life to the full, she is nevertheless saddened by the sense of loss that accompanies living to such a great age. She has a lively circle of much younger friends, many in their seventies but many my age and younger, with whom she socialises on a regular basis. It doesn't bother them that Mary is twenty, thirty or even forty years their senior; her mind is still that of a young woman. At her birthday party she surprised us all by producing a limited edition book which she had written on a recently acquired computer, beautifully bound and presented. Part memoir laced with imaginative fiction, it's a series of short stories, essays and anecdotes drawn from her life, presented as a timeless gift to her children, grandchildren and great-grandchildren (of whom there are eleven).

Looking at my stalwart mother-in-law, I'm prepared to admit that I have neither the genes nor the lifestyle to reach the age of ninety. And I seriously question that I want to. David is eleven years my senior and we regularly discuss the pros and cons of the ageing process. For someone as usually positive as me, I take a negative view. For someone as usually negative as David, he takes a positive view. David is working on himself to remain as youthful and healthy as possible. He watches his diet, has shed more than 20 kilos in the last five years and goes to the gym almost daily to keep up his cardiovascular health and flexibility. He has late-onset diabetes, which he controls admirably with diet and exercise, and his blood pressure and cholesterol are fantastically low. At sixty he was delighted to receive his Seniors Card and regularly quotes from the small print on the back: 'The holder of this card is a valued member of our community. Please extend every courtesy and assistance.' In 2004 he turned sixty-five and pronounced with some pride that if he wasn't still working he would be eligible for the pension. I winced ever so slightly at the prospect of living with a pensioner, ashamed at my own attitudes which may appear ageist but in fact are based on fear.

My father committed suicide at sixty-two. I resolutely believe it was because he was terrified at the prospect of growing old. His lifetime of heavy drinking and smoking had taken its toll on his physical appearance and health. He suffered from undiagnosed depression, and after the dissolution of his marriage to my mother, sparked by the latest in a twenty-five-year string of infidelities, he was in a frame of mind where he saw no future for himself. Like most of his actions in life, his decision about his death was purely selfish. At the time, I was not distraught at the loss. He had been such a difficult person to deal with in life that his death seemed to me, then twenty-two and pregnant with my first child, a blessed relief.

Now, in my mid-fifties, for the first time I feel compassion for my father's plight. I am saddened that he was incapable of sharing his fears about ageing with his family and that he saw his future purely as his own to deal with. Not as part of a family unit. Although he had niggling health problems, it wouldn't have taken that much of a lifestyle adjustment to haul himself up and live for another twenty years or more. He chose not to.

That said, I fear I have similar thought patterns to those of my father when it comes to ageing and death. It alarms David when I mention my penchant for 'living hard and dying young'. I take a rather fatalistic attitude to the whole thing. I'm not saying I'm right – and the medical profession would clearly argue against me – but I somehow feel that taking the cautious approach may ironically not pay off in the end. How disappointing it would be to live a life of rigid self-denial, constantly worrying about healthy lifestyle, diet and exercise regimes, only to be struck down by some unexpected disease in mid-life. It certainly has happened to various friends of ours, while others we know who lead dissipated lifestyles soldier on well into their eighties. I hear the words 'moderation in all things' ringing in my ears, but my natural inclination is to be excessive. To push the boundaries. I'm not advocating a life of total self-indulgence, but I cannot tolerate the prospect of total self-denial.

It's all relative. When I mention my fears about ageing to my mother-in-law she has every right, but doesn't, to laugh out loud at me. As do the women in their sixties and seventies I regularly meet at talks and book events. From their perspective I'm still young and shouldn't waste my time dwelling on old age – just as teenagers never for a moment contemplate the prospect of turning thirty-five. But fifty is the threshold. It's the point at which we first start to focus on ageing and mortality, to look back and reflect on our life and to ponder the prospect of the future.

In France, many of my friends are over seventy because the tranquil rural paradise of the southwest attracts lots of retirees. My friends Jock the retired journalist, Claude the English ex-photographer, and Margaret Barwick the garden designer and author are just some of those in our circle who are twenty years or more older than me. But they don't behave as though they are twenty years older, with their high spirits and a full-on approach to life that belies their years.

Jock's method of dealing with ageing is to ignore it completely. It's not a bad philosophy in many ways. Denial is a great form of self-protection and it means that Jock simply dismisses the signs and signals that tell him it might be time to slow down, and he continues to behave like a man half his age. Most of us find it hard to keep up with Jock's predilection for socialising. It's not uncommon for him to throw his enthusiasm into a restaurant lunch that lasts from noon until well after four in the afternoon, then rest for an hour or so before going down to the bar or the Plan d'Eau to have a glass of Perrier for the purposes of rehydration before an evening of more eating and drinking and general merriment. He bowls up to all the weekly fresh produce markets in the local villages, loves to fossick for old bits of china and glasses at the antique and flea markets that are the highlight of the summer, and throws at least one four-course dinner party a week. He's an exhausting person to be around.

Apart from his wheeze, the legacy of a lifetime of asthma, he seems in robust health most of the time. In more recent years he has, however, developed the alarming habit of dismissing any indications of ill health – such as a cold that may have turned into bronchitis or, worse, pneumonia – by always saying, when asked by concerned friends, that he's feeling a lot better than he did the day before. This is usually just hours before he admits that he is actually feeling quite distressed and unable to breathe, which means that he must be rushed to the doctor or hospital for emergency assistance. In other words, he waits in the hope of a miracle recovery until he is virtually on death's door before acknowledging that he could be quite ill.

While this positive and hearty attitude is preferable to being a neurotic hypochondriac, it can be quite unnerving for those asked to assist in a crisis. Claude recounts with some horror driving Jock to Prayssac to see the long-suffering local doctor – then immediately, at speed, driving to the hospital in Cahors with Jock literally gasping for each breath in the passenger seat.

Claude was convinced he would be dead on arrival and was therefore amazed when he returned the following day to visit Jock only to find him sitting up brightly in his bed tucking into the substantial regulation hospital lunch that includes a small bottle of red wine.

Mentally, Jock is as sharp as ever and his wit and comic timing remain unchanged, making him one of the most sought-after dinner party companions in the region. He has, however, become a bit vague about details and sometimes forgets if an invitation has been issued, especially if the request has been made in the middle of a lunch or dinner when the wine is flowing. A lot of us fall into the same trap. The social scene is so casual that engagements are not written down and therefore are often not remembered. It's not that uncommon for Jock not to show up and the host or hostess to call and ask, 'Where are you, Jock? We are about to sit down.' And for him to reply, 'I wasn't invited.' Then quickly pick up his car keys and head for the door.

Jock's performance with cars and driving in recent years has also been somewhat alarming. A year ago he totalled his trusty Peugeot driving home after a long lunch when his foot slipped from the brake onto the accelerator while he was parking outside his ancient stone cottage in the late afternoon. His version of events was that 'the house reared up in front of the car', and the result caused much mirth among his circle of friends, although for Jock it meant forking out for a new (second-hand) Peugeot, as he was not covered by comprehensive insurance.

This year's incident involved my house and the car of our mutual friend, Anthony. It was the first night of the Frayssinet village fête – a four-day extravaganza of music, food and family fun. The first evening event was moules frites (meal of mussels and chips) in the salle de fête (community hall) behind the mairie (town hall) opposite my little village house. I was in Australia at the time and so have to retell this tale second-hand from those who were witnesses.

A table of more than twenty had been organised by Miles and Anne, who live just up the road from the mairie in a substantial old farmhouse, Le Clos, set back from the road in a large rambling garden. The plan was for people to leave their cars in the mairie car park and walk up to Le Clos for an aperitif or two prior to the meal. Jock arrived on time and left his car outside the mairie. Anthony arrived quite a bit later and, finding the car park full, decided to tuck his Land Rover safely into the narrow space between my house and the derelict house next door. I often park my own car in this handy spot when in residence.

At eight o'clock the group walked down towards the salle de fête and noticed Jock's car parked at an awkward angle outside my house. More than awkward – indeed, it was sticking precariously out into the road. On closer inspection it was discovered that the car had escaped from its original parking spot and careered across the narrow but always busy road, where it had crashed into Anthony's smart vehicle, removing the bumper bar and numberplate, before bouncing unceremoniously into the corner of my house (only a fraction away from my newly planted deep purple clematis). The back of Jock's car was quite badly smashed about and both lights were wrecked – another huge garage bill to add to the ongoing expense of the summer. His new car was an automatic and the general consensus was that Jock had not managed to put it into 'park' or had forgotten to pull on the handbrake. He insists that there must have been some outside intervention – perhaps he had parked in the wrong place and some irate local had let off the handbrake to teach him a lesson.

When I phoned from Australia the next morning, having heard the bad news on the grapevine, he simply reported, with his usual wry delivery, 'It hasn't been a good week. The septic backed up into the garden and the upstairs loo stopped flushing. The phone line doesn't work and the computer's fucked and won't do emails. Then the cat died. Now this.'

Apparently that same evening, much later after the meal, our Scottish friend Sandie – who now lives near St Caprais permanently after retiring from her job as a window-dresser in a smart Edinburgh department store – reversed her car over a three-metre embankment and had to leave it there and get a lift home. It was retrieved by the local mechanic, Monsieur Molieres, with a truck and chain the following morning.

Sandie's only comment on the whole affair was that it was a shame that Anthony, who is a keen paraglider, didn't have his 'flying contraption' in the back of his car at the time of the accident. 'Then Jock would be one of the few people in history to have succeeded in colliding with a car, a house and an aeroplane all at the same time,' she quipped.

I believe, from reports, that a 'survivors' lunch was held at Le Clos the day after to celebrate the events of the night before.

The rest of the weekend fête was fairly low key and incident-free. They had peaked early.

14

After I meet the publisher's deadline for finishing *Last Tango* in January 2003, life at home on the farm somehow slips back into an almost normal routine. David and I have stopped talking quite so obsessively about the affair and its aftermath – the book – and the fact that later this year we will have to deal with the publication and the possibility of a lot of negative publicity. We simply try to get on with our lives without dwelling too much on our problems. In any event, when I am home in Australia, France seems like a distant dream. A fantasy. And even though I know my recent trips have caused unholy havoc in my life, it still doesn't seem very real. It's another world, totally removed from my real life.

I am getting organised to return to France in May for a second walking tour and David is continuing to develop various film projects that are not without frustrations and setbacks. Over the years I have learned to be realistic about the ups and downs of the film industry. It sometimes takes a decade for a project to get through all the developmental stages, from early script to final draft, finding the right director and cast, then pulling together all the money for the actual production. So I tend to switch off from the day-to-day irritations David experiences in his work as a producer. There just seem to be endless obstacles to be negotiated and egos to be smoothed. I suppose it's a natural part of a process that involves such creative collaboration, but I have developed a fairly cynical outlook and don't allow myself to get excited about a film until it is actually in production. David takes my attitude as a lack of interest in his career, but my view is that I don't allow myself to get caught up in the emotional rollercoaster of the business – I just enjoy the fruits when they finally ripen.

In February we decide to take a driving trip to Adelaide, where David has two new film partners and where he has also been invited as a guest of the local film festival. Driving is a great way for us to have some time out for ourselves, away from the pressures of computers and faxes and phones. We often have our most serious and constructive conversations in the car – also some of our worst fights, but at least we are cocooned from the world as we drive along admiring the diversity of the Australian countryside. During this trip, the drought is particularly apparent as we drive down through West Wyalong and then over the vast Hay Plains to Renmark, where we spend the night. We walk around this beautiful town on the Murray River and have a great meal in a local cafe, sharing a bottle of wine.

At times like this we are totally happy together and I wonder why our marriage has been floundering so badly. David is convinced that I am harbouring anger and bitterness from my perception that he let me down badly as a husband and father during the decades he was so focused on his career, almost to the exclusion of all else. I believe, however, that while those short-comings certainly caused me pain and resentment at the time, I am well over them now, that our problems have more to do with the 'here and now' of our relationship and its continuation into the future.

I am still clinging to the hope that I can keep up the juggling act. Have my cake and eat it too. The fact that I can sit here in a restaurant with David having a lovely time, laughing and drinking wine and going back to the motel to make love, all the while knowing that I have recently embarked on a second affair in France, is utterly confusing to me. How can I do it and feel okay about myself? Have I finally uncovered a fundamental flaw in my character that has been dormant all these years? Am I turning into my father – the man of whom I have always been so critical, a serial philanderer who did what he wanted to pleasure himself without apparent thought or concern for the feelings of others?

I don't sleep very well any more and it's not surprising. I usually get off to sleep okay but wake in the middle of the night and spend an hour or so contemplating life. Not just my own messed up situation but life in general. My children and grand-children. The world, poverty, pollution. Refugees and the fact that human kindness is on the decline. The fact that we now seem to care more for our bank balances than our neighbours. I have turned into a mid-life midnight worrier, and it shows on my face every morning.

Perhaps it is normal that at this stage of our lives we start to worry more about broader issues. When our children are no longer our responsibility we widen our concerns. Look at the big picture. I know that a lot of my friends report the same night-time restlessness. Or could it just be that as we age we seem to need less sleep?

One night during the dark hours before dawn I contemplate the nature of love. I recall so vividly my first love as a teenager. How utterly overwhelming the sensation, how completely I drowned in it and allowed myself to be swept along. I recall too the love I felt for David in our early years together. Not quite as intense as first love but certainly deep and satisfying. I felt protected and secure and this was reinforced by the birth of our first two children.

Motherlove. There are no words to describe the force of it. The love of a child leaves all other loves behind in its wake and remains a permanent, lifelong fixture. As a mother it becomes obvious that it is possible to love more than one person at a time. I recall being fearful when pregnant with my second child. Worrying how I was going to find love for this new baby when I was already so much in love with our firstborn, our daughter Miriam. I even went into labour worrying, but my fears were instantly allayed at the moment of Aaron's birth. Here was the same love all over again. No less potent.

Grandchildren also bring their own love in spadefuls. It's overwhelming. I can sit at the dining room table with the entire menagerie and look from face to face with the confident knowledge that I love every one of them totally. And David too. How fortunate am I.

Could it be that I can love more than one man? Two perhaps, or even three at the same time? Could I move easily from one to another, without remorse, savouring the individual and special relationship that I have with each? Does sexual love have to be exclusive? Just as I am able to love each of my children individually, am I also capable of loving various men in my life without one relationship detracting from another? Each lover has offered something different and unique. Can any one man give a woman all the things she needs (or would like to have) from a relationship? Can any one woman totally satisfy a man?

Of course I am not the first woman to contemplate this complex issue. I read with fascination the fictional prose and memoirs of Anaïs Nin, who in the 1940s was doing things that I have never even dreamt of. As I read her books I am amazed at how similar we are in our thought processes. A few years back I would have read her books with distaste, regarding her as both selfish and immoral. Now I have an insight into her passion for life and her desire to explore so many possibilities. She writes so poignantly about her love for her husband and in the same breath about her compelling attraction for other men. Her words jump off the page at me. I could have written them myself:

'The impetus to grow and live intensely is so powerful in me I cannot resist it. I will work. I will love my husband but I will fulfil myself.'

A *Spy in the House of Love*, Anaïs Nin, 1952

Was her behaviour outrageous and self-destructive? Or had she liberated herself from the constraints of convention and opened her heart and her mind and her body to all the excitement that life has to offer?

I also loved reading Nigel Nicolson's *Portrait of a Marriage*, about his mother Vita Sackville West's adulterous affairs yet never-ending love for her husband Harold Nicolson. And the writings of Charmian Clift about her love affairs and lifelong bond to her husband George Johnston. These stories haunt me.

Am I just wildly trying to justify my behaviour? I don't know.
I don't know anything any more. I like to think I am in control
of my life but I am dangerously on the edge of a precipice and
at any moment I could fall.

15

While we are in South Australia I get a call from my publisher's publicist, Jane Novak, to say that the ABC's 'Australian Story' would like to film a program with us. They have been sent an unedited advance of *Last Tango* and are interested in making a documentary on the contents of the book. Jane assures me that it is entirely up to us, but that it would be good for the book if we agreed. Very good.

I keep the request to myself for a day or two while I mull it over. I know David will be less than enthusiastic and I don't want it to spoil our time away. Back at the farm, I broach the subject with David and he responds exactly as I would have expected.

'Don't be mad, they will crucify us,' he says. 'You've been working in the media long enough to know the story they want. They'll just want to highlight the affair.'

I know he's probably right but I go ahead and phone the researcher, just to test the water.

A very pleasant young man talks to me about the book. I ask if he has read the first book and if he knows the rest of the story.

The lead-up to my leaving for France in 2000. The discovery of my long-lost sister Margaret. My family background. The suicides and alcoholism.

'No,' he says, 'but I will do so immediately.'

He seems keen to get his head around the whole story.

A few days later we talk again. I explain in some detail that we are very concerned that the story will place too much emphasis on our troubled marriage and the affair mentioned in *Last Tango* and not give enough weight to other aspects of the saga.

He assures me this isn't the case. That they are keen to shoot a balanced account of our recent life mingled with all the background and colour described in both books. He promises it won't just be a beat-up about a grandmother who went to France and had a fling.

David is still very resistant to the idea. He is convinced we will have no control over the content of the film and that they will manipulate us to get the story they want. We both have a great respect for 'Australian Story' and love some of the programs they have made over the years. But of late we are of the opinion that they have gone downmarket, choosing subjects more for their sensational value rather than for the worthiness of their subjects. Like David, I fear we fall into the sensational category.

In talking with David about the pros and cons of being filmed, I point out that it would be churlish of me to write honestly and candidly about our lives in my book then refuse to discuss it any further with the media. I also point out that we are going to have to face all sorts of questions and interviews when the book comes out and that surely, of all the media, 'Australian Story' will be our best opportunity to get our viewpoints across.

David reiterates that he would prefer to 'maintain a dignified silence'.

After continued lengthy discussions with the researcher, however, we progress to the next stage, which is to meet with the proposed producer, Janine Hosking. Janine has won awards for her work and has a great reputation as an honest filmmaker. We meet her separately – she comes to the farm for a day to see me and discuss the program and then she has a get-together with David a few days later while he is in Sydney at meetings. We both like her. I trust her, but David is still less than confident that we will be presented in a balanced light. However, Janine assures us that she will do her best to represent us fairly and not produce a beat-up.

The timing is to be critical because I am leaving for France in less than five weeks. The ABC needs to spend about ten days filming with us, and I realise our life will not be our own between now and when I get on the plane. But I feel quite comfortable that Janine will tell the story with integrity. David still has grave reservations about the whole thing.

'Just imagine how this is going to be for us,' he says. 'Instead of putting the whole episode behind us, we are dragging it on and on. First with the book and now with the film. It's madness.'

He is right, of course, but I'm not prepared to admit it to myself. I see our differing perspectives as a representation of our opposite personalities. David always taking the negative view. Me always taking the positive. I rationalise that if the book sells well it may in some way compensate for the pain it has caused.

With hindsight, totally skewed logic.

16

Our lives are invaded by the 'Australian Story' film crew. Anyone who has been involved in the making of a documentary will know what it's like, and we of all people should have realised the time implications of saying 'yes'. David's experience as a filmmaker and my nine years with 'Gardening Australia' have given us much more insight than most, but even so we are shocked at the intensity of the invasion.

It's a small crew. Just the producer Janine, the cameraman and a sound recordist. They stay in nearby holiday cabins and arrive every morning immediately after breakfast. We film all day and they rush back to look at what they have captured before going to bed early to recharge their batteries for the following day's filming. It's exhausting. We retreat to our bedroom every night feeling shattered. The interviews alone take four or five hours, and they are done individually so neither of us really knows what the other person has said. Although we certainly have a pretty good idea.

Janine wants various members of the family to be interviewed.

I ask the children, but only Miriam agrees. The boys are not camera-shy but the notion of being questioned about personal family problems worries them. My stepson Tony, who is married and lives in Sydney, has been very level-headed about our marital problems, not taking sides or passing judgement and offering love and support to us both throughout. But my biological sons Aaron and Ethan have been more deeply affected by the events of the last few years. In a sense my behaviour and its aftermath have rocked the foundations of their lives, having always felt secure in the belief that their parents were an unshakable unit. Perhaps they fear showing pain or anger during the interview and we don't blame them at all for declining to be involved. Miriam, on the other hand, has plenty of views and attitudes that she would like to express, and in a sense almost relishes the opportunity to speak out.

Janine would also like my sister Margaret to record an interview for the program in Canada, but I feel certain she will refuse. Having her long-lost little sister reappear in her life after fifty years has been confronting enough for Margaret to cope with without the emotional strain of being interviewed for a television program as well. I give her the opportunity and she declines. As I expected.

Janine is keen to capture the beauty of the farm and the surrounding countryside, and she is fortunate to have the talents of a particularly gifted cameraman, David Marshall. It's autumn and they shoot scenes at dawn in the rolling mist and at sunset with the house nestled among the old exotic trees. It's cold so I light the open fires, which fill the rooms with a glimmering warmth that is also captured on film. I try to keep my input as lighthearted as possible. I make jokes and brush aside questions that I consider too intense or deep and meaningful. The only time I am moved to tears is when I talk about finding my sister Margaret. I had been determined not to cry, not to give way to such a public display of emotion. But I can't help myself.

Janine wants to film me leaving for France. She wants to capture the moment of our farewell as I pass through the wide doors to the customs hall. David and I debate the issue all the way to the airport.

'She doesn't want us to act,' I keep saying to him. 'She wants the real thing.'

He is adamant that after we embrace and say our goodbyes for the camera I must go through the departure doors and wait a few moments before returning to say goodbye properly. Privately, without a camera under our noses.

David feels that the film is robbing us of a private farewell and is therefore too much of an invasion.

I check my bags through and fill out the customs forms. Our body language is nervous and hesitant, which is surprising because we have been filmed for weeks non-stop and surely by now we should be appearing relaxed in front of the cameras. But we are like wound-up springs, because in truth this moment will be the most significant in the film. David holding me before I leave once more for my other life. My fantasy life. For France.

When we embrace it is slapstick in its exaggeration. David insists on a full passionate kiss and I feel self-conscious and awkward. I disengage myself from his arms to go, aware always of the camera behind me. I turn for an instant and wave, then disappear behind the screen. I wait fifteen seconds and walk back to David and hug him again, properly. We have our private moment but I quickly retreat. The whole business has been too much for both of us and I can't wait to escape the prying eye of the camera.

But for David the ordeal is still not over. As he walks away from the departure doors, the camera picks him up and closes in on his face.

'How do you feel about Mary going?' Janine asks.

'Anxious,' he says. 'I'm always anxious when Mary is flying. I won't relax until I know she's safely arrived.'

'No, no,' she continues. 'That's not what I mean. I mean, how do you feel about her going back to France?'

'In what sense?' he says.

'Well, surely you can't trust her?' A probing question that catches him by surprise.

'I'm not going there, Janine,' he replies. 'That's not something I'm going to respond to.'

But she has hit a raw nerve. He already has a feeling that things are not quite right between us. That there is more to the story than I am telling him. Obviously the instincts of Janine, the documentary maker, are also alert to the fact that the story is by no means over yet.

17

Why do I love this place so much? Why do I feel so good when I am here, so far from my family and all the people and places that have made up my life for the past fifty-four years? The pleasure I get in opening up the house, unlatching the shutters and letting the spring sunshine pour into the main room. Making up the bed with clean sheets and then cleaning the house from top to toe because it has been closed up now for seven months. I throw open the bedroom windows and shutters on the first floor and lean out over the road. I see familiar faces coming and going from Hortense's corner store, the alimentation that provides the village with the convenience of all sorts of produce from fresh Roquefort cheese to Bordeaux red wine, available from breakfast time until sunset every day. I love the familiar stone tower of the old church, cracked as it is but with a new shingle roof, and the bells that chime on the hour and half-hour, twenty-four hours a day.

I see Madame Thomas shuffling down the road towards the boulangerie. She is now walking with the aid of a stick, so perhaps she has had a fall since I was here last year. Then again she must be quite an age now and the winters here are pretty gruelling, so it's not surprising she suffers from aches and pains. She looks up and sees me at the window, smiles and waves enthusiastically. I feel so happy. So welcome. So much at home.

This year I plan to paint the inside of the house white, to brighten up all the corners that are dark and dingy. The new kitchen looks perfect, but I also need curtains to give me privacy from the main road and to seal off the house in winter, because I have a tenant coming after I leave at the end of summer and I don't want her to have to endure the cold from the draughty gaps in the front windows and shutters. Curtains will certainly help.

There is no May walking tour this year because the dreadful Bali bombings and the SARS scare have made Australian tourists temporarily nervous. But we have lots of bookings for September and in the meantime I intend working on a novel. My first attempt at fiction writing and therefore rather daunting.

David is staying back at the farm until May, when he leaves for his annual pilgrimage to the Cannes Film Festival. This year in June our daughter Miriam will celebrate her thirtieth birthday, and as a special treat we have bought her a ticket to visit us in France. Her husband Rick has agreed to take three weeks off work to care for their four boisterous boys, two of whom are at school. Rick's father, John Parsons, will come down from Queensland to Bathurst to help him. After a decade of being a full-time mother, this will be Miriam's first real break from domesticity and she is filled with excitement but also has some qualms because she is anxious about missing the children.

Miriam has been to France twice before – once when we took all four of our children on an extended overseas trip that included two months in Provence, and once when David had a film in competition at Cannes and I was unable to be there to support him because, just days before the festival, my mother Muriel had a stroke. The ticket had been paid for so we sent Miriam instead, and as a fifteen-year-old swanning around the Côte d'Azur she had the time of her life. Now, fifteen years later, she is returning and I can't wait to introduce her to the delights of this region and the joys of living in the village.

David, however, is ambivalent about coming to Frayssinet. It will be his first time back here since the affair and he is sensitive about it. He sees the house and the village as a representation of his pain and unhappiness. He believes that the house is my place, not his, and that I used it not only to escape from him and from our marriage but to launch myself into an affair. In some ways he's correct, but I am constantly trying to encourage him to see things from a different perspective. To look ahead rather than always dwell in the past.

In my heart, however, I know that whatever I might be saying to David is totally compromised by the secrets I am keeping from him. On the one hand I am encouraging him to 'get over it' and 'move on', but I am also keenly aware that I have betrayed him yet again and that my words are filled with hypocrisy. All I can say is that when I talk to David about working to repair our marriage and about staying together I sincerely mean it. When I tell him I love him, I mean that too.

On the plane from Australia to Paris, I spend a lot of time wondering what will happen when I return to the village. I have maintained sporadic email contact with my new lover since last year but we have communicated only about inconsequential things, with no mention from either of us about our relationship. Is it over or will we pick up the threads again this year? How do I feel about it? Confused as ever. All I keep saying to myself, over and over, is that David must never find out.

Within hours of arriving in Frayssinet, I find myself down at Le Relais catching up with my gang of friends. Christian and Christiane greet me like a member of their family. The local barflies smile in recognition and kiss me on both cheeks, after first removing stubby cigarettes that seem permanently stuck in the corners of their mouths. Jock arrives, then Claude. It is a wonderful reunion. Locals wave a welcome greeting as they drive around the intersection. It's a strange feeling, almost as though I haven't been away at all. I am quickly filled in on all the latest news. The boucherie/charcuterie has closed down over the winter, which is a tragedy for the villagers. Didier, the butcher, also has a thriving shop in Cazals, but the man who has managed it for him over many years left suddenly and Didier could not find a replacement. Unable to keep two businesses going by himself, he reluctantly closed down the Frayssinet shop.

Didier was also facing the prospect of having to spend a lot of money to upgrade the Frayssinet shop to bring it up to European Union health standards, which have been imposed across France. Traditional boucheries engage in all sorts of practices that no longer conform to European norms. In the old days fresh meats and prepared foods, such as terrines and foie gras, were all displayed together in one glass cabinet. Now, separate display units with regulation cooling must be provided. The floors must all be standardised for cleanliness and even internal architectural details, such as the old oak beams that are an attractive feature in many old shops, must be covered over completely. One of the charms of the village butcher shop has always been the weekend rotisserie with rolls of chicken and turkey and pork that are placed outside mid-morning, filling the air with the rich aroma of spit-roasted meats. This is also being phased out, along with the giant paella pans that steam with the smell of rice and saffron and fresh prawns cooking.

Given that most of Didier's customers were the elderly people of the village, there simply wasn't enough cash flow from the business to spend on all the obligatory renovations. So the building was sold, to be converted into a gîte (holiday apartment), and now the locals must make do with a butcher's van that sets up twice a week in the car park. Many of the older locals don't have transport to get to the larger towns for markets or to the supermarket. So instead of buying fresh meat every morning for the tasty lunches she makes for herself and her husband, Madame Thomas must plan ahead and shop on Wednesday and Friday afternoons instead.

Hortense at the alimentation has been similarly affected, and the rumour is that she will close down completely within the next year or so. This will be a disaster for the village. Apparently the health inspectors have been and the list of requirements for her to satisfy their demands is as long as your arm. For decades she has been selling everything from cleaning products to cat food, from tobacco and wine to fresh fruit and vegetables and of course local cheeses and processed meats such as ham and salami. Hortense has a round table in the corner of her shop, and when her friends pop in to visit they all sit down and have coffee and cake and a good old chinwag. She's now not allowed to drink coffee in the shop or entertain her friends, which makes life tough for her because she is open almost ten hours a day. So far she is ignoring the directive.

Hortense and her husband Jacques have three small dogs who also hang around the shop all day. They often sleep on the plastic chairs outside in the sun and they make a daily pilgrimage into my courtyard and stand at the back door, longingly hoping for the scraps left over from my last evening's meal. I usually reward them. When the weather is cold, they huddle under the table inside the shop where Hortense and her friends sit chatting and laughing. This is now an absolute no-no. No animals are allowed anywhere near a shop that serves fresh produce. I recall when I first moved into the house and Hortense had an old cat that slept all day on the shop counter on the pile of newspapers she used for wrapping various purchases, pulling sheet after sheet from under the dozing moggie. The cat on the counter never worried me, but imagine the look of horror on the faces of the inspectors. Just as well the cat has since died!

Hortense will first dispense with her cold food cabinet because it no longer complies with the standards. So there will be no more cheese or ham or fresh milk or yoghurt. Then the racks of vegetables and fruits that she wheels out in the morning will have to go unless she is prepared to resurface the floor and line the timber-beamed ceiling. All that will be left is tinned food, wine and tobacco. Such a shame.

18

Within days of returning to France, I have resumed my heady relationship with my lover from the previous summer. We didn't broach the subject via email while I was home in Australia, but the moment we meet again it's as though there has been no separation. We both know that David will be arriving from Cannes soon and it's as though we are trying to condense as much as we can into the few weeks that are available to us.

Unlike my previous affair, which was conducted well away from the village over long flirtatious lunches with breathless anticipation, this is much more clandestine and constrained. We are careful not to be seen out alone together, for the obvious reason that it would initiate gossip. So we carry on with our usual routines and meet at times when we hope nobody can observe us. Our paths sometimes cross in social situations because we have friends in common, and those evenings are quite tricky because we mustn't allow our body language to give the game away. Making eye contact, knowing that we will be seeing each other later, is quite thrilling for me. And if we accidentally touch it feels like a jolt of electricity passing through my body.

Yet emotionally I feel quite differently about this relationship. I am capable of being more objective. Of standing back and analysing what is happening. I am keenly aware that for me it's very much a journey of sexual experimentation and discovery. I'm a middle-aged woman and a grandmother and here I am exploring aspects of myself that I never knew existed. Playing sexual games and being adventurous. Is it the sheer danger of it I enjoy? I realise I am taking a great risk, but I am mesmerised by the excitement and simply cannot resist the temptation of continuing.

My lover also maintains a certain distance, and this is strangely one of the attractions. Instead of smothering me with words of love that could easily smack of insincerity, he says very little. It's all in the eyes. There's a driven quality to our lovemaking, a certain desperation. I am aware that I am still on the rebound from having terminated my relationship with the man from Toulouse, and that part of the pleasure is the pain of it. At times I see us as two rather lost and unhappy souls clinging together for mutual comfort, and at other times I see us as two knowingly irresponsible adults behaving very badly indeed.

The problem is that I have lost my perspective. I'm too much in the here and now, and not considering the bigger picture of my life and my relationship with my husband. It seems easy to dismiss everything that has been my world up until now and just live for the thrill of the moment. In the situation I'm in, it suits me to take the view that we were never really meant to have just one sexual partner for life. That it's only natural for a woman to evolve sexually, just as she does intellectually and emotionally, and to therefore desire different partners as she matures. I've conveniently forgotten that my sexual life with David always has been, for me, the most crucial aspect of our long and often difficult relationship. It bound us together through the challenges of rearing children and balancing demanding careers. It was more important to me than anything and now I've just thrown it away for the sake of immediate gratification.

I'm getting very little sleep, often driving home at some ungodly hour half-dressed and trying to sneak back into the house without waking up the entire village and setting the tongues a-wagging. I stick to the back roads to avoid encountering the gendarmes who sometimes mount late-night patrols at village intersections. Instead I drive along the winding narrow roads through the woods, encountering strange wildlife in my car headlights. Huge white owls, deer and weasel-like creatures that scurry along the side of the road. The last thing I want is to have a conversation in broken French with a curious gendarme at 3 a.m. with my underwear spilling out of my handbag. I usually coast down the hill to the car park with the engine off and the lights dimmed, then wait until there is complete silence before gathering myself together and tip-toeing across the road to my side door. If I catch a glimpse of myself in the large mirror in the main room, I see a dishevelled and disarrayed figure. My lover always phones to make sure I have made it home okay. It becomes a nightly ritual. It's all sheer madness.

On the phone to David I am acting out the role of busy French housewife, getting the house in order and stocking up the pantry for his arrival and also for Miriam, who will fly down from Paris the day afterwards. It's a charade.

In spite of our best efforts, eventually there is some gossip within our circle of friends and my lover and I become aware of it. I have always assumed that the French don't give a damn about the private lives of their friends and neighbours. That they are too civilised to chatter about other people's peccadilloes. After all, isn't 'taking a lover' supposed to be a normal part of the French way of life? No doubt just another myth that they have to live with. In any event, the gossip isn't among the villagers, it's within the expatriate community and it's rather unpleasant. It seems that some people in our circle are always on the lookout for a bit of scandal. My lover is an eligible bachelor, somewhat sought after by some of the single women we both know. And I am a married woman on the loose. One person has seen my lover and me in the wrong place at the wrong time and put two and two together. The odd ambiguous remark is dropped over drinks and dinner. Soon the whole place is abuzz with it and we can't help but be aware by the way people stop talking when we walk into a room, or huddle in a tight conversation, then look at us. I am totally unaccustomed to this type of situation and I really don't have a clue how to handle it. So I revert to type and bury my head in the sand, hoping that if I ignore it, it will just go away.

In the meantime, relations between David and me are extremely strained. He has arrived in Cannes and is engrossed in his usual round of meetings and parties. When we speak he sounds wound-up and anxious, as though he's not really enjoying himself. This is not customary, because usually David gets a total charge out of being at the Festival and thrives on the business of it. This time he just sounds exhausted and irritable. Several times we exchange cross words for no particular reason other than that we are both obviously stressed. He keeps saying that he is dreading coming to the village. That he really doesn't want to be part of the scene any more. My response is that he shouldn't come to Frayssinet if he's feeling so negative, but he's determined to be part of Miriam's birthday holiday. He says it's the only reason he's coming and this makes me sad. I really want him to like it here and to feel part of the place. By his attitude, it seems unlikely that he ever will.

By late May the weather has started to become hot. Unlike Australia, where spring and autumn are quite long seasons, here the weather seems to go from freezing cold to stiflingly hot in just a few short weeks. When I first arrived, I was lighting the big Godin fire downstairs to warm up the house in the early morning when I was having my first cup of tea. I would sit toasting my toes in front of the oak logs in the grate, staring bleary-eyed into the flames and trying to get a grip on my life. But by the time David is due to arrive from Cannes, it has begun to get very hot and I have stripped the doonas off the beds and started closing the shutters in the middle of the day to stop the bedrooms from becoming overheated.

By now I am actually looking forward to David's arrival. My reckless behaviour is catching up with me physically and emotionally, and I hope that when David arrives there will be some stability and I will be more centred. After all, he is my partner of more than three decades. He has a steadying influence on me and I certainly need a little steadying at the moment. There's also the fact that I want him to love the house and to feel at home here. To stop seeing it as 'my' place and start thinking of it as a place where we can both have a lot of fun during the summer months. Perhaps with Miriam staying with us, David might relax and begin to enjoy a more positive frame of mind.

I spend time making the house look as welcoming and homely as possible. Jan lends me various bits and pieces from her attic to brighten up the main room – lamps and pretty mirrors and paintings, mostly originals that she has done herself, to hang around the walls. Philippe lends me an old wooden chest of his grandmother's for storage in the bedroom. Margaret Barwick gives me two handsome pale blue chairs that really make all the difference to both the comfort and the appearance of the small sitting area. I want the house to remain quite simple – not too cluttered or over-decorated. And I am very mindful that I need to keep a lid on the budget. The house is already costing us a lot more than we anticipated.

The night before David arrives, I visit my lover for the last time. We haven't discussed it, but we both know that from this moment everything must stop. I just turn up on his doorstep, very late, and he is waiting for me. I don't feel any guilt or shame and I have no regrets that it has come to an end. He will still be my good friend – hopefully we will always remain friends.

How should I be feeling? I honestly don't know. Tonight is tonight and tomorrow is tomorrow. For me, strangely, they are in no way connected.

19

 My life has always been one of walking that delicate line between responsibility and rebellion. At school I was more often than not the model student. A prefect. The editor of the school magazine. A member of the debating team and the person chosen to speak on behalf of the student body on Anzac Day. But I also smoked in the toilets, occasionally nicked over the road to the wine bar for a Cinzano and lemonade at lunchtime, and wagged school in the afternoon to meet up with my long-haired dropout boyfriend. In my final year my prefect badge was stripped from my lapel because I announced an anti-Vietnam protest at the school assembly.

As a parent I joined the P&C Association, served in the school canteen, worked hard as a school fundraiser, and enrolled my children in a multitude of extracurricular activities including sport, music, languages and art. But I roared with laughter when they swore and behaved outrageously, and in their teens I tolerated them smoking dope and having their girlfriends and boyfriends to stay the night. I let them turn one of the bedrooms into a disco where they graffitied the walls and had all-night music sessions.

In my career I have also swerved between the respectable and the outrageous. I have worked as a social reporter covering weddings and picnic race meetings for an upmarket women's magazine, and I have written dozens of articles about the joys of pruning roses. But I have also edited a local newspaper that was so scandalous that at times our lawyer used to tear his hair out in disbelief at some of the articles we attempted to publish.

So there probably have always been two versions of me. The 'good' me who conformed to expectations and managed with good humour huge amounts of responsibility. And the 'wicked' me who has always been lurking just slightly under the surface, wanting to rock the boat and ruffle the feathers.

Like most journalists I have always aspired to the fantasy of one day becoming a publisher, knowing full well that the reality of achieving the lofty heights of a Rupert Murdoch or Kerry Packer is highly unlikely. Despite the ethical notion that publishers have absolutely no say in editorial content, any journalist who has worked for a large newspaper or magazine publisher knows that there is an 'editorial policy' that comes from the top. The ultimate power.

Although my bread-and-butter income during the twenty-five years we lived in the Blue Mountains was as a gardening writer and editor, I always retained a fascination with mainstream journalism, devouring all the newspapers, from the national dailies to the weekly local rag.

One icy Katoomba evening in the late 1980s I was invited out to a trendy cafe for dinner by an old friend who had published a weekly newspaper in the upper Mountains for several years.

This had, to his financial and personal disappointment, been sold out from under him by his business partner. In his frustration he'd come up with the idea of starting his own local monthly newspaper as an independent publisher, and was curious to see if I was interested in being involved – not just as the editor but as co-publisher. On every level it was a crazy idea. Financially potentially disastrous in an environment where there were already two well-established local newspapers. There simply wouldn't be enough advertising dollars to go around. Who would work on the paper and how would we pay them? We would need writers and photographers and advertising sales people, not to mention computers and production staff to do the design and layout. It was sheer madness but I leapt at the idea, convincing David that it was financially feasible if we recruited supporters who were prepared to give their time without pay. I must have caught him at a weak moment because he agreed. The *Blue Mountains Whisper* was born.

My publishing partner in this hare-brained scheme was Geoff Fanning, a London printer who had migrated from the UK in the early 1980s with his glamorous blonde wife Anna and their son Jan, who had a peaches-and-cream English schoolboy complexion and a charming accent compared to my rough-and-tumble youngsters. Geoff had the wackiest sense of humour I've ever encountered. Because his trade as a scanner operator bored him rigid, he balanced his life by writing comedic essays and sketches, which he later performed as stand-up comedy routines on the live comedy circuit. In essence, Geoff was a frustrated writer and photographer, and therefore part of his motivation in wanting to own his own newspaper was as a forum for his creative energies. One of his first forays into getting his humour in print was by writing regular letters to the editor of the entrenched and highly conservative weekly *Blue Mountains Gazette*, which he did under a pseudonym. It took the naïve editor quite a while to realise that letters from J. D. Castleberg were a hoax, but in the meantime they created a stir in the local community. His tongue-in-cheek humour was over the head of some people and so the letters were always being discussed in coffee shops and offices around the Mountains.

The only way to make the *Blue Mountains Whisper* work was for it to be different in style and content from the two main-stream newspapers and to rally as much unpaid assistance as possible. The Mountains have always been a haven for creative people – writers and artists and musicians – and it was up to us to enthuse them with the concept and to get them involved.

The biggest political issue in the area at the time – both on the state and local government level – was the destruction of the environment by thoughtless and greedy overdevelopment. So we decided our paper should be a pro-environment/anti-development newspaper with a strongly satirical bent (this was Geoff's forte). Our first target for help was Greg Gaul, a local artist/cartoonist, who we hoped would design a masthead and set the style for the paper. He immediately agreed, lured by the challenge but also by a promise of regular meals around the kitchen table and a good supply of my homemade beer. He was fantastic and his wife Carol, a teacher, was also enthused by the concept.

Quickly others came on board. I talked to Richard Neville, who shared our outrage at the environmental destruction happening on a daily basis right across the Mountains. He and his journalist wife Julie Clarke both offered to contribute articles.

Noni Hazelhurst, before her days on 'Better Homes and Gardens', was also keen to write a column. Designer Jenny Kee, always at the forefront of environmental battles, contributed and local writer Ken Quinnell volunteered, along with two computer whizzes who could do the layout using desktop publishing. Essentially this technological breakthrough was what made self-publishing feasible for people like us. Until computers could be used to design and lay-out pages, the cost of production was prohibitive. Now it was possible to put together a sixteen-page newspaper in less than a week using the new design programs, and we could also design and lay-out advertisements. All we needed were people who would buy space, and this task fell to a local woman, Susanna Miller, who agreed to chat up local businesses and take only a commission. My brother Dan, also a journalist, offered to help with the first few issues. It was all hands to the pump.

The other Mountains papers were give-aways and we would have to charge at least $1 a copy just to cover printing costs. We didn't worry about not earning an income from the paper, but we certainly didn't want it to cost us money. At the time I was editing a series of bi-monthly gardening magazines, so we organised our *Whisper* deadline to fit in between my 'paying' obligations. Geoff had a city job with a printer, so we had enough income to survive if our crazy scheme didn't take off immediately.

What followed the launch of the *Whisper* were the most outrageous and funniest three years of my life. The kitchen table became the editor's desk, and regular meetings of contributors were held in and among family dinner times. My mother, also an old journalist, loved the buzz of these editorial think-tanks, but erred on the side of caution, always fearful that we would be sued. Glass of Scotch in hand, she would wave her arms in dismay at many of our story ideas – especially ones that involved holding local politicians and public figures up to public ridicule. We ignored her advice, taking the 'publish or perish' point of view.

We attacked the local aldermen on council, the state government ministers and the opposition as well. We quickly managed to offend just about everyone – left-wing, right-wing, religious, conservative, feminist, arty, greenie – no group or individual was spared our scrutiny and undergraduate humour. Our local Liberal state member, Barry Morris, was a rotund man in his fifties who, several years after the *Whisper* days, was sent to Berrima jail for making threatening phone calls to a local alderman. Barry had a reputation as a bit of a bully boy, but we found him utterly benign. He was fond of his food, our Barry, and we frequently bumped into him at public events or functions that involved eating. Barry was always the first in line at any community sausage sizzle, so we established an editorial policy of only publishing photographs of him eating. It wasn't difficult to achieve – Geoff and I carried our cameras with us everywhere and Barry even played up to the joke, posing with a slice of cake or a handful of hot chips every time he saw us approaching. He didn't seem to feel at all threatened by us, unlike most of the other local politicians, who took our lampooning far too seriously.

Getting the paper out every month was very much a family affair. My mum proofread and subedited the pages and reiterated her dismay at some of our more outrageous articles. David wrote a film column, Miriam posed for photographs for advertising and Aaron, wearing a baseball cap with the word 'Shithead' on the crown and a plastic dog turd on the brim, stood beside the then Liberal premier Nick Greiner while he was opening the annual Leura Fair. It made for an hilarious photograph. Mum (once more against her better instincts) even agreed to be photographed for our bumper Christmas edition in bed, clutching a flagon of sweet sherry, with Geoff dressed in a Santa Claus suit, with the headline 'Santa Strikes Again'.

Geoff took photographs and wrote various columns, including a restaurant review and his regular 'Wasted Days' monologue, which developed a bit of a cult following. Sydney broadcasters such as Margaret Throsby and David Spicer would regularly quote from our pages on morning radio.

Amazingly, we did get good advertising support from local business, including one of the most prominent real estate agencies in Katoomba, and we managed to cover our costs with enough left over for the odd bottle of wine or two.

Sad to say, eventually our high jinks got us into trouble – serious trouble in the Supreme Court, with a defamation suit slapped on us by three local politicians who failed to appreciate the humour of our scribblings. It didn't stop us – in fact it made us even more outrageous, but eventually we ran out of puff because of time commitments. All of us needed to have 'proper jobs' to keep the wolf from the door, allowing less and less time for our *Whisper* antics. The defamation suit was settled out of court (thank heavens we had good insurance) and the *Whisper* faded away, we like to think with dignity.

It certainly was one of the most creatively charged and high-spirited times of my life, and thinking back to it reminds me of the naughty streak that I have never really managed to suppress. And that, eventually, being naughty will get you into trouble!

20

I drive to Agen to collect David from the train. Ever since we have owned the house David has caught the train to Toulouse after the Cannes Film Festival and then connected with a train to Cahors so I can pick him up. But it's a bit of a logistical nightmare because David always carries far too much luggage and there is less than fifteen minutes between the connecting trains. He has to wrestle his bags down steep stairs from one train, find a departure board to locate the platform for the Cahors train, then make a dash for it. Both previous times he has only managed to catch the train by a whisker and has arrived in a state of nervous exhaustion.

So I make some investigations and discover that there is a through train from Cannes to Agen, which is a slightly longer drive for me but far less of a hassle for him. I have only ever driven to Agen once, so I relish the thought of exploring the different countryside again. Agen is famous for its prunes, which are used in so many ways: prune tarts, prune liqueurs, prune sauces, rabbit and quails sautéed with prunes, and prunes soaked in eau de vie which is a regional delicacy.

It's a beautiful day and the scenery is outstanding. Vast fields of sunflowers just coming to a head, patches planted with maize, and endless vineyards with small stone villages punctuating the countryside. The architecture changes as I drive south and the region appears to be more prosperous than the Lot, where I live. I am trying to feel happy at the prospect of having David and then Miriam arrive, but somehow I fear it isn't going to be an easy time for us. David is still incredibly fragile about the man from Toulouse and I fear it will sit like a cloud over our family holiday.

I have taken time with my clothes and make-up and I am hoping we can manage a happy reunion. Throughout our marriage we have spent long periods apart, mostly because of the nature of David's work. The best part has always been getting back together again. The reunion. I haven't seen David since that stressful afternoon at Sydney airport with the ABC film crew in our faces, and although I know he will be tired from the long hours that are a part of the Festival, I am hoping he will be in a slightly more positive frame of mind.

He falls out of the train with his usual quota of oversized bags, plus numerous smaller carry bags stuffed with scripts and magazines and Cannes paraphernalia. He is being assisted by a tall man who carries several of the bags. As I walk towards him, anticipating an embrace, he just nods at me and continues an animated conversation with the man. I stand waiting and eventually the man moves off. David looks frazzled and gives me a cursory hug.

'Who was that?' I ask, imagining that it must be someone he knows, perhaps also from the Festival.

'Just a man from the train. He spoke English and offered to help me get off.'

I feel somewhat deflated. The moment has been lost. We just haven't made an emotional connection and it's as though, from the very start of our holiday, the tension has set in. Driving through the glorious countryside I make attempts to point out landmarks, but that does nothing to lighten the atmosphere. Eventually I challenge him: 'What's your problem?'

And his anger pours out. He doesn't really want to be here. He never wanted to return to the village. He's only coming because of Miriam. Under sufferance. Nothing I can say will make any difference.

It's obvious that we are in for a difficult summer.

Even when we arrive at the little house his mood is leaden. Resentful. I have filled it with flowers and the courtyard looks pretty in the dappled evening light. But he just wants to collapse and drink gin. He's carrying tobacco and rolls himself cigarette after cigarette. He hasn't smoked – except perhaps two cigars a year – for thirty years, and I can see that he's using these as a crutch. A coping mechanism. But in reality the alcohol and tobacco make him even more wound-up and stressed.

We make love in a desultory fashion. He's tired and I'm annoyed at his negative attitude. I'm now wishing he hadn't come after all. That he had just left the film festival and gone to England, which was an alternative he had proposed during one of his unhappy phone calls from Cannes.

The following morning we drive to Toulouse to pick up Miriam, who will have endured the gruelling 34-hour trek from Bathurst via Paris. I wish we could have had a few days to resolve our differences before her arrival, but the plan has always been for her to be here on her thirtieth birthday – which is in two days' time. We arrive before her plane is due to land and are astonished to see Miriam already standing at the entrance to the airport looking anxious. She is overwhelmed with relief to see us, because the journey has been a nightmare. In Paris there was a baggage handlers' strike and her luggage was lost at the terminal. The connecting plane to Toulouse was cancelled, so she was rushed by coach to another airport to pick up a Toulouse flight that actually arrived 40 minutes ahead of the one she was originally scheduled to take. She's tired, frazzled and dirty and has no clothes, just a small Air France emergency pack that contains face cream, a toothbrush, disposable knickers, a tampon and a condom. They have promised to send her bags on by taxi.

David does the driving and I point out the various châteaux and churches nestled on the hillsides as we wind our way from Cahors to Frayssinet. Her spirits start to lift as she takes in the absolute beauty of the countryside, with the old stone houses that remind her so much of the one we rented in Grasse when she was a child. It's after lunchtime and I immediately drag her across to the bar and start introducing her around to the locals. We order the largest beer we can get – more than a pint – and she gradually starts to calm down and look around her. Jock, Sandie and Gordon appear from nowhere, and within minutes we are laughing and talking thirteen to the dozen. Miriam looks around the square, at the church and the streetscape with its colourful bar awnings and tables and chairs spilling into the roadway.

'Oh Mum, this is an amazing place,' she says. 'I can see why you love it here so much.'

21

The long hot summer begins in earnest. Miriam and I formulate a plan of the things she wants to see and do. She has only three weeks, including the two days travel at each end, and while she wants to see as much as possible she also wants to chill out a bit because it's the first time in ten years she's had a holiday without children. She's interested in sight-seeing, but really only the towns and villages in quite a small radius. She loves the markets and wants to see as many of those as possible, and she also wants to meet all our friends and socialise. She would love a couple of days in Paris but we have decided we can't afford that. Perhaps we will spend a few days in Toulouse at the end, before putting her back on the plane.

Her bags are not delivered by the airline within the promised 24 hours so she will be eligible for some insurance compensation for the purchase of emergency clothing. We dash into Cahors and do the boutiques, which is great fun, especially as there are sales on and lots of amazing bargains. French clothing, especially the ranges designed for young women, is comparatively inexpensive and always well made from good fabrics, as well as being stylish. She buys gorgeous new underwear, some groovy jeans and tops, a lovely skirt and a new pair of shoes. This is an unexpected bonus as we never anticipated buying a new wardrobe as part of her holiday.

Everyone is keen to meet her, so a series of lunches and dinners and drinks parties are organised. She ignores her jetlag to keep up the pace and gets into the swing of the local scene instantly. We go to the Prayssac market and buy cheeses and cold meats and crusty bread for lunch. Her eyes roll back in her head as we devour the goodies spread across the kitchen table.

'I'll never be able to eat cheese in Australia again,' she declares after sampling the Roquefort and Cantal. 'It will be a total waste of time.'

Miriam and her husband Rick are foodies and both are great cooks, so she is fascinated by the range and variety of foods available, not only in the markets but also at the supermarket. We spend hours trawling the shelves and she gasps in delight at the jars of terrines and tins of foie gras and vegetables – especially the slender haricot vert (green beans) that are quite different from the French beans we grow and buy in Australia. The meat section is particularly fascinating to her. The meat is often butchered differently, with unusual cuts available and delights such as breast of duck and leg of rabbit just sitting there on the shelf. So much more exciting than a boring old lamb chop! The sausages are also very different – thick rich red Toulouse saucisse curled up in a circle, and rows and rows of duck and pork salami-like saucissons.

Miriam makes the observation, quite accurately, that there is hardly anything available apart from traditional French ingredients. There are some pastas from Italy and a few other foreign staples such as couscous and rice, but very little that is exotic. In Australia we have become accustomed to a wide mix of south-east Asian ingredients being readily available. I point out that the French are quite chauvinistic about food, protecting their traditions by limiting the availability of ingredients from other cuisines. It's possible to get bits and pieces to make a curry or a stir fry, but there simply isn't a great diversity.

There is, however, an entire row in the supermarket devoted to wine and spirits, and the cost of the alcohol is amazingly low compared to Australia. We stack the trolley with reds from Bordeaux and Bergerac and rosé from Provence and Spain.

This is paradise for Miriam, and she's sad that Rick isn't along to share the delights. But, surprisingly, she hasn't started missing the children as yet.

'Give me time,' she says. 'I'm having too much fun.'

The village house is quite small, without much privacy, and even though we are going out and about a lot, we are also spending quite a bit of time at home together. In spite of our efforts to avoid confrontation, Miriam naturally picks up on the tension between us and handles it by making jokes. She must have inherited that strategy from me.

'God you two, get a life,' she says as we snipe at each other over some trivial matter. 'Now I remember why I left home.'

I feel mortified that we are spoiling her holiday by being so unhappy together, but privately Miriam reassures me that it's fine. She's having a great time.

We organise a birthday party for her, and luckily the weather is hot and sunny so our guests can spill out from the main room into the courtyard. Miriam enjoys the pleasure of preparing for a party using all the local delicacies – we visit the market in Prayssac on Friday morning and buy cold meats, pâté and cheeses including Cantal, Camembert and the best quality Roquefort we can find. There's a stall that just sells olives – from tiny black Kalamata to plump green varieties that have been marinated in chilli. Smoked salmon is good here, and we also buy a large quantity of red capsicums so I can grill and skin them and soak them in good Italian olive oil. The tomatoes are at their peak and have a flavour that you simply never taste in tomatoes at home unless you grow your own. We slice them with basil and make a large green salad using all the leafy varieties that are plentiful in the market.

In the village we order a chocolate gâteau and a fruit flan from the patisserie, which is considered to be one of the best in the district despite the fact that our village is comparatively small and remote. We buy our crusty bread here, too, rather than at the markets because, once again, the quality is impossible to beat.

We invite people for midday and the house quickly fills with noise and laughter. It's a great way of celebrating her birthday – and it's not lost on me that Miriam is our first-born and very much our love child. It all seems so long ago when I look back and recall how young and carefree I was at the age of twenty-two, when she was born. Life was so uncomplicated then and I was happy, truly happy, with my love for David and my secure place in the world. How confused and contradictory my life is now by comparison.

Every day is crammed with places to visit and people to meet. We take Miriam to the thirteenth-century bastide town of Villefranche-du-Périgord to see the little room in the back of a shop that I rented during that first summer of my escape. We walk down the ancient back streets and admire the medieval architecture that remains intact everywhere – towers and court-yards and decorative doorways with flat iron nails. Miriam loves the hotel in the square with its weathered stone archways and the covered market with its stout stone pillars, famous as the centre of the cèpe trade in the autumn. These knobbly mushrooms are highly prized and plentiful in this region and the town is overrun with eager buyers every Saturday morning. They are used fresh in omelettes and also preserved in glass jars for use in stews and casseroles all through the year. They have a distinctive flavour and texture – quite different from truffles – and I just love them, even though they can be quite expensive.

We also visit Montpazier, which is one of the most popular bastide towns because of its unspoiled central square, often used as the location for television dramas and films set in medieval times. There are excellent shops here and we buy some presents for Miriam to take home for the children.

Most days Miriam and I head for Le Relais in the square for an aperitif before lunch. We are usually joined by friends – Jock of course, but also Claude or Jan and Philippe if they happen to be passing. While we are socialising, David is generally power-walking, choosing to stride purposefully through the woods for several hours to compensate for the fact that there is no local gym where he can get his daily exercise. He refers to the walks as his 'punishment', which indeed they must be because the weather has really started to warm up and he arrives home dripping with sweat and very flushed from the intensity of the activity. He tells me it's his thinking time, apart from anything else, and a good way of redirecting his angst about being here.

I find his attitude difficult to deal with, just as he finds my nonchalance infuriating.

It's tempting for Miriam and me to sit too long and drink yet another glass of rosé in the summer sun, but eventually we tear ourselves away and prepare lunch for the three of us. We all tend to snooze in the late afternoon, then there's usually some sort of social event in the evening – a new restaurant to try, or a dinner party with friends.

'I don't like the lifestyle you live here in France,' David says. 'All this non-stop eating and drinking and staying out late. I just can't keep up the pace, and you will have to understand I just don't want to be part of it all the time.'

To lighten the atmosphere, I make jokes about David being 'boring' and a 'wet blanket'. But I certainly don't intend staying home quietly every night. And I point out that, as Miriam is here for such a short time, we must make the most of every minute.

David's negativity saddens me, but I also understand how he must be feeling. I love this place so much and sense he is punishing me for what happened here last year by resisting my entreaties to lighten up and enjoy himself. I want him to get over it and move on. Stop dwelling in the past. Totally unfair of me in light of the secret I am keeping.

Several times we find ourselves at dinners and lunches also attended by my lover. Sitting at tables laden with wonderful food in friends' lush summer gardens. Laughing and drinking the afternoon or evening away as though nothing untoward has been going on between us. Weirdly, it doesn't make me feel even slightly uncomfortable – in fact I am always delighted to see him. I suppose I should be feeling odd with my lover and my husband sitting at the same table, talking and drinking together. But I don't. I try to avoid direct eye contact and certainly any give-away body contact, but I still manage to find myself sitting between them on more than one occasion.

It may seem bizarre but in fact it doesn't rattle me at all. Perhaps because we were friends before any of this happened, I am capable of slipping back into the 'just good friends' mode. Or perhaps I subconsciously enjoy the frisson of having my lover and husband at the same table. Or it could be that I have managed to package my life and my emotions into separate portions. Right now I am in a family phase, with Miriam visiting and David in residence. Only two weeks ago I was in a single woman phase, enjoying all the freedom that that entails.

Miriam laughs and says that it feels very strange to be living back under the same roof as her parents. She left home at seventeen to go to university in Canberra and hasn't really lived at home since, except for a couple of brief spells between moving houses. Without her husband and four children to look after, she has slipped back into her old role as our dependent daughter.

'I feel like I'm reverting to my childhood' she laughs. 'I love sleeping in a bit, and the fact that you two are doing all the washing and cooking. It's just like being a kid again.'

What I fail to realise during Miriam's visit is that David is gradually gaining an awareness of what has been going on while I was here alone – both last year and before he arrived this year. He has no firm evidence and says nothing at all to me, but his pain and anger are simmering away under the surface and this has a profound effect on the atmosphere in the house. I can't explain how it feels, but Miriam surely also senses the explosive mood. David is drinking furiously and still smoking non-stop, which is totally uncharacteristic. One night in bed we have a whispered fight, trying not to upset Miriam, and he leaps out of bed and starts getting dressed, saying that he is leaving immediately. That he can't tolerate being here one more moment. I beg him to calm down and to stay, which eventually he does. But it's a strong indication that things are very rocky indeed.

The days fly past and suddenly we realise there's less than a week left of Miriam's holiday. We decide to spend some time in Toulouse, even though the temperature is rising to the high 30s and a heatwave has been predicted.

Toulouse is a beautiful and elegant city. The streets are wide and tree-lined and the buildings are constructed of the local pink stone, which is quite distinctive. There are classical ornamental parks and gardens, and squares lined with outdoor cafes and restaurants, and the shopping is mind-boggling. But the whole place also has a youthful vibrancy because it is very much a university town.

Miriam is immediately enchanted. After the tranquillity of our rural village, the energy of Toulouse captivates her. David does the driving and I navigate us into the city, where we find a comparatively cheap hotel in a narrow back street. The tariff includes parking. It's almost unbearably hot and we stagger to find a cafe where we can sit and recover from the drive with a cool beer. In the main square, Place Wilson, we stumble across a street parade with people dressed in the most outrageous costumes. Men dressed as women and women dressed as men. Suddenly, reading the banners, we realise it's a Gay Pride March and we find a shady cafe, sit down and watch the whole performance.

We have some memorable meals in Toulouse, which is much more cosmopolitan than the rural area where our village house is located. We eat Spanish, Italian and Chinese cuisine, and blitz the shops, which are also of a much higher standard than those in the small towns and villages. Not that we can really afford to do a lot of shopping, as we have already far exceeded our budget and will need to live a bit more frugally once Miriam leaves for home.

'This has been such a great experience,' says Miriam. 'I'll never forget this holiday – it's been fantastic.'

I start to feel unhappy about Miriam leaving. Apart from missing her because we have had so much fun together, I will now have to deal with David on my own and I sense it's not going to be easy. We have another six weeks together, and while I initially hoped it would be fun, I now fear it's going to be a nightmare.

We farewell Miriam tearfully and drive back to Frayssinet in virtual silence. The three days in Toulouse were exhausting, not just because we were keeping up with Miriam's exuberance but because the temperature gauge never dropped below 40 degrees. The French heatwave of 2003 has begun.

$$22$$

 In late June 2003 the temperatures across Europe start to climb rapidly and by mid-July they are hovering daily in the high 30s. While it's usual for most parts of France to experience high temperatures in July and August, this particular summer is much, much hotter for much, much longer than any summer on record.

In rural France the summer heat is dry, like inland Australia, and therefore more tolerable than the humid heat experienced in other regions. But this summer is not just hot, it's breathless. There are no breezes to bring relief in the still of the evening, and even during the long twilights the temperature barely drops a degree or two.

During previous summers in France I have experienced several weeks of heat followed by much cooler spells and some blessed rain. This year, hot days turn into hot weeks which turn into hot, hot months. It is relentless.

Our village house faces south and gets sun on the front wall from mid-morning right through until the evening. The dark bitumen road abuts the house, with only a narrow concrete footpath barely 60 centimetres wide as a buffer between the house and the road. There are no patches of green lawn or shady trees to soften the impact of the sun. It just beats down on the house, punishingly, day after day. The trucks roll past belching diesel fumes that seem more caustic than usual, and tractors laden with bales of hay also rumble past our front windows on a regular basis. It's hot and noisy and dusty and quite different from the previous summers I have spent here.

The walls of the house are more than a metre thick, and normally this ensures that the interior remains cool even on the hottest summer day. But not this summer. During July, the stone gradually soaks up the heat from the sun as well as the reflected heat from the roadway. It becomes like a heat bank, storing it overnight and into the following day. I am advised by the village women to keep the heavy timber shutters closed from sunrise to sunset. It certainly makes a difference, but it means that the house is in constant darkness. The windows inside are left open in the hope of a welcome breeze that may flutter through the cracks and gaps in the shutters. But the breeze never comes. Inside the house it just gets hotter and hotter, so that by August it's much cooler outside in the courtyard at midnight than anywhere in the house itself. Sleeping becomes an ordeal.

I try to buy an electric fan to make the bedroom more tolerable at night, but they have sold out everywhere. Weeks ago. Bottled water is also scarce on the supermarket shelves and when a new batch is delivered there's a frantic rush to buy up whatever stocks are available.

The heatwave is a crisis all over France, but news of its devastation is slow to filter through the media. And for us, living without a television and rarely reading the local newspapers, there is total ignorance of what is going on in the wider world. The weather reports about the heatwave are consistent, but it will be many weeks before we get news of the alarming death toll.

The heatwave is all anyone talks about. Locals are glued to their television sets at night, anxious for news about the weather. Desperately hoping for a storm or a cooling change to come through. People are only venturing out in the early mornings or the evenings, and nobody wants to sit on the plastic chairs and tables outside Le Relais except late at night. Even Madame Murat's restaurant, normally packed at lunchtime during the summer, is eerily half-empty except for the road workers and truck drivers who are obliged to keep working despite the conditions. It's just too hot for the rest of us to contemplate a huge five-course lunch and all that red wine in the middle of the day. Heaven knows how Sylvie and Madame Murat manage in the kitchen, deep-frying frites and baking roasts of veal and lamb. It must surely be unbearable.

But holidaymakers seem to be enjoying the hot conditions, especially those from England where days and days of hot sunny weather are such a rarity. They sit out until midnight in shirt-sleeves, drinking beer or chilled wine and relishing the almost tropical atmosphere. During the day they sleep or sit wherever there is some shade – in stark contrast to the local farmers and other manual labourers, who have to endure the beating sun on their backs all day long. It's a very trying time.

The inescapable heat adds to the tension in our relationship. We both seem strung out, and David is exhausting himself by insisting on continuing his obsessive exercise regime, often walking in the middle of the day when the sun is at its hottest.

I buy bulk rosé from Bergerac and we bottle it together over the sink, hammering in the corks and stacking it in rows inside the fridge, which is struggling to stay cool. It's often too hot to eat very much, but we still manage to get through the rosé, using it as a prop to dull our fragile senses. We seem to spend half the day numbed by wine and trying to avoid getting into an argument. The topic of our relationship becomes taboo. We are just getting through each day the best we can.

We get a message from home that the 'Australian Story' episode we made is being screened in July, not September as agreed with the researcher and producer at the time of filming. David is beside himself with rage. The agreement on timing is important, because he wants to be back in Australia when it is screened so that we can be with our family, as a unit, to face it together. There is also the issue of the book, which won't be released until October – the original agreement was to time the documentary screening as close to the book release as possible.

We are also told that there have been problems with the edit. The producer, Janine Hosking, has presented her version of the story and it has been rejected by the executive producer. We can only assume this means one thing: Janine has made the film we agreed to and it has been knocked back by management. They want the story they want. It's an editorial decision.

We try talking to the executive producer but it's like banging our heads against a brick wall. We get nowhere. She is adamant that the program will be broadcast as soon as it's finished.

I have always loved the ABC and have watched it almost exclusively since my parents bought our first television set in 1961, when I was eleven. Our children were only ever allowed to watch the ABC, never commercial television because I hated the ads. For nine years I worked on contract with the ABC on 'Gardening Australia', although that experience left me feeling rather disenchanted towards the end, because management decided that merchandising products to align with the program was a great marketing idea. None of us – the presenters – wanted a bar of the commercialisation of the program and our attitudes have been vindicated in the long term because most of the products, apart from the magazine and books, failed to find a market.

The ABC prides itself on being a public broadcaster, providing a public service with its programming. They are not, they claim, driven by competition for ratings with the commercial networks. They only present factual, balanced programs and never sink to sensationalising subjects or to participating in celebrity beat-ups. That's what they claim, anyway.

Not only did the ABC break their verbal agreement with us to screen the program in September, but they sent tapes of the show to the tabloid weekend newspapers to get as much advance publicity for the Monday night screening as possible. Quite apart from the fact that they eventually edited the film to concentrate almost exclusively on my troubled relationship with David and the affair I had written about in *Last Tango*, they exploited the 'sensational' aspects of the film to their own ends.

The weekend before the screening of 'Something About Mary' – the tacky name they had decided to call the episode – Miriam phones us from Bathurst to read us the tabloid headlines.

'Hope you're sitting down, Mum,' she says.

David is listening on the other extension.

'Listen to this one: "Garden Guru in Torrid French Affair".'

I gasp in disbelief. Then dissolve into helpless laughter.

'It gets better, Mum. "Gardener Admits Adultery".'

David is ashen-faced. He isn't laughing. He is very angry and outraged by what has been written.

As a journalist I can see the humour and absurdity of the situation. I recognise the stupidity of tabloid headlines – I have been responsible for some myself in my days as a journalist on *TV Week*. But this is patently ridiculous. Any integrity that the ABC may claim to have in the standard of its filmmaking for this program has been thrown out the window. The whole handling of the situation has been shameful.

'Australian Story' goes to air and we speak immediately with the children. Miriam is crying. While she and Rick found most of the film okay – perhaps not the balance David and I would have liked, but certainly beautifully filmed and put together – she is distraught that her closing line in the interview has been edited.

The question was put to her: 'What have you learned about your parents through this whole business?'

Her response was simple: 'I have learned that my mother can be more selfish than I ever thought she could be – but then again that's not a bad thing because she has spent all her adult life being unselfish and giving to others. And I have learned that my father can be more loving and tolerant than I ever thought he could be.'

They had cut out the second line. The line about her father. And she felt as though the words had been cut out of her mouth with a sharp knife.

The simple truth is that when you hand over your story to be made into a film, you have absolutely no control – and maybe, in some ways, that is not such a bad thing. An outsider can look at a story objectively and tell it through different eyes, take a different perspective. When I am writing, I have total control over what I say and how I choose to present my story. I always try to be honest and truthful but it is all subjective. It is my story, but only through my eyes. Not the eyes of an outsider.

We agreed to do the program and so it's a fair cop. Janine did an outstanding job of making a beautiful and for many people a quite poignant and moving film. David Marshall, the camera-man, won an award for his fantastic work on it, and overall I have to say it was compelling television.

One question remains. Should it have been made at all? Was it, within the guidelines of the program, a subject that justified the time and money spent on its production? A lot of people don't believe so, and with hindsight I think they are correct.

A filmmaking colleague of David's takes a very dim view indeed. His comment is: 'What's the ABC thinking about, making a film about a high-profile media couple and their fucked-up marriage? It's a waste of taxpayers' money, and a waste of airtime.'

Given that the producers didn't stick by their original under-taking to tell the 'whole story' and instead opted for highlighting only the sensational aspect of the affair, I think he's probably right.

24

 The days are getting hotter and we are drinking even more rosé than ever. My plans for painting the house interior are shelved because it's just too breathless to paint. It's really too hot to do anything. After fifteen minutes up a ladder the sweat is running from my scalp down the back of my neck and I feel dizzy and exhausted by the sheer effort of even setting up the equipment and stirring the paint. The persistent heatwave has sapped everyone of their energy and those with any sense stay inside most of the day, only venturing out when the sun drops low in the sky.

The house has become like a sauna, and it's very difficult to sleep at night. Some nights I dampen the top sheet and lie under it in the hope that a breeze may flit through the bedroom window, which is open wide all night. Friends tell me that they have abandoned their upstairs bedrooms and have taken to sleeping in the salon or even in the courtyard. Often the only cool place in a house is the cellar, and I hear that plenty of people have dragged mattresses down into these dark rooms

normally used for storing wine and cheese. Our cellar is too
small and dirty to contemplate sleeping in, so we persist in
sleeping in the bedroom despite the discomfort.

Various friends have swimming pools and we sometimes fall
into these at dusk. If we go to the markets we only go first thing
in the morning, and long hot lunches are almost totally off the
agenda. We live on salads and cheese and foods that require little
or no preparation.

A week after 'Australian Story' has been aired, I am sitting in
Le Relais at lunchtime drinking a cool beer with my friend Miles,
who is down with his wife Anne for the rest of the summer. An
English couple sit down at the next table and start chatting. They
are house-hunting and are finding the relentless heat exhausting
as they are shuttled from one village to the next by the eager
real estate agent. Against the front wall of the bar I notice a man
sitting alone, also drinking beer. David suddenly looms into view,
flushed in the face and dripping with sweat from his fast and
furious power walk. He stops and joins us and we order a jug of
rosé, which he proceeds to drink on an empty stomach. Not a
very wise idea. As we talk, the man from across the road walks
over to our table and asks if I am Mary Moody.

'Yes, I am,' I reply, with some curiosity.

'I'm a journalist from the London bureau of the *Sun Herald*,
in Sydney,' he says. 'I've been sent here to find you and to talk
to the locals and establish the identity of the man from Toulouse.
Do you mind if I join you? Let me buy you all a drink.'

We nearly choke on our drinks and sit wide-eyed in stunned
disbelief.

I ask him to repeat what he has just said because, quite
honestly, I am finding the whole notion impossible to get my

head around. Surely, surely, a journalist wouldn't travel all the way from England to this isolated little village in southwest France to follow up such a silly story? It's just too ridiculous for words. I tell him that I think he's wasting his time and ours. But I find it difficult to be rude to him or to send him away with a flea in his ear, even though it probably would be the best idea. As a journalist myself, I recognise his dilemma. No matter how foolish the story, he has accepted the assignment and has come a long way (at the expense of the newspaper) to follow it through. He has to come up with something.

With some embarrassment, Miles leaves us to our predicament and the English couple at the next table look rather confused – they obviously realise something unusual is going on, but can't quite work out the significance. I've had no breakfast either, and by now I am on my fourth drink and feeling very woozy.

'Look,' I say to the reporter, now feeling rather sorry for him, 'this whole thing is a complete waste of your time. Do you speak French?'

'No,' he says.

'Well, the people around here don't speak English, so how do you intend interviewing them? And how will you find the man from Toulouse when he doesn't even live around here? It's a joke, the whole thing's just stupid.'

David says very little and keeps pouring himself rosé.

'Apart from anything else,' I add, starting to get a little angry, 'the whole concept of a story about us is a waste of paper, a waste of column inches. Who gives a damn about us and what we do in France? We're grandparents. We're old people.'

'That's right,' David adds. 'We're not Tom and Nicole.'

'Well, I have to write a story no matter how silly you think it is,' says the reporter. 'So you might as well give me your point of view. And it doesn't really matter if I find out the identity of the man from Toulouse or not, as long as I file a story some time today.'

The heat and the wine make the whole scenario seem even more surreal. I suddenly realise that David and I are quite drunk and probably also in a state of shock. I decide to somehow rescue the situation.

'Why don't you join us for lunch?' I ask the reporter. 'We'll answer your questions and then you can go back to London.'

So the three of us, David and I weaving, cross the road to the house, which is in darkness from being shuttered all morning. I open it up and quickly throw together a large platter of cold meats, cheeses and salad. Fortunately I had already bought our daily loaf of crusty bread because the boulangerie is now closed for siesta. The reporter falls gratefully on the food and gets out his notebook and pen. David foolishly pours more cold rosé from the fridge.

As we eat I start to feel slightly better and more in control of the situation. We answer his questions and I realise that he hasn't been briefed properly and knows very little about the background to the story, only some sketchy details from the Sydney office of the newspaper. He knows nothing about us, which is just as well from my point of view because I can therefore give him our perspective. Ultimately he is so grateful that we haven't slammed the door in his face and are not only being co-operative but also quite hospitable, that I hope he will file a story that isn't salacious.

As he leaves, he asks if he can take a photograph of us outside the house. He pulls out a tiny camera which is very non-threatening, as though he's just taking a family snap. I don't know why we agree to this, but it seems harmless enough. We are standing on the hot road – me barefoot – both with a glass of rosé in our hands. He clicks the camera once, smiles, thanks us and disappears back to Le Relais, where we learn later he's been staying for the last two nights.

We never see him again.

Next Sunday, Miriam phones again. 'You're in the *Sun Herald* again this week,' she says, obviously highly amused. 'There's a whole double page spread story and a huge photograph of you outside the house. You both look drunk. And you'll never guess the headline this time, "A Tangled Tale of Tango in Toulouse"!'

Great.

I feel as if we have dreamt the whole thing. How did this happen to us? We are the most unlikely candidates for all this media attention. All I can think is that the Sunday papers must be totally desperate for stories to devote two pages to a couple of middle-aged to elderly grandparents going through a marriage crisis. I wonder what my Dad, who for nearly twenty years edited the *Sunday Telegraph*, would have thought of the whole thing. He would have laughed, I'm sure.

25

The summers of my Australian childhood were all beaches and boats and cricket. Living at Balmoral, my brother Dan and I regularly went for an early morning swim at 'the net' before school and spent every weekend and all the long summer holidays in the sun, ignoring our painfully raw, burnt and peeling skin by revelling in the sensuous pleasure of the golden sand of the harbour beaches and the endless and glorious blue skies.

Although quite protective of us as young children, once we could swim competently my mother simply let us go. The beach and its environs were ours to explore unsupervised, and often we would leave first thing in the morning and not return until sunset. We set off with little more than a towel and a sandwich and an apple for lunch. We drank water from the bubblers, and sometimes we had sixpence for an iceblock. Quite early in the piece Mum despaired of giving us a tube of zinc cream to protect our noses and shoulders from the relentless sun. We invariably lost the tube and managed to get burnt regardless. We were cautioned to sit in the shade in the middle of the day, which we usually did because the sand was unbearably hot – too hot to lie on. But our skin was also remarkably tough. I could walk over sharp rocks and gravel pathways, and even the bubbling bitumen on the road surface didn't daunt us particularly – the soles of our feet were like leather.

Both Dan and I were strong swimmers because at the tender age of five we were automatically inducted into the Balmoral Swimming Club. The summer I was due to join the club I was still not comfortable swimming out of my depth, so a neighbourhood mother decided to take the situation in hand by leading me out to the deep end of the baths where the races were held every Saturday afternoon. She piggybacked me down the ladder and swam with me on her shoulders out to the centre – about six metres deep – then abandoned me. It was sink or swim, so I swam. To the nearest ladder, which was about 25 metres away. The following Saturday I was entered in my first race – in those days twenty-five yards, which was half the width of the baths – and by the end of the season I was swimming in three or four events every week. These days, the notion of throwing a nervous non-swimmer in the deep end would be considered child abuse, but in the 1950s it was the expedient solution to my fear of deep water. It worked.

Cricket also dominated the agenda – not just the Saturday morning suburban competition games my brother Dan played but the after-school backyard games in which I was sometimes allowed to be involved. There were lots of neighbourhood kids who loved a hit, among them a tall, good-looking boy, David Colley, who would go on to become a well-known state and national cricketer. He and Dan were the closest of mates, despite the fact that in childhood Dan was a chronic asthmatic who spent a good deal of time gasping for air.

Although they were of a similar age, David was bronzed and broad-chested, towering over Dan, who had the translucent skin, sunken chest and dark shadows under the eyes that characterised asthma in those years before preventive medication. But his comparative frailty didn't hold Dan back in the cricket department. He was tough and wiry and more than determined to keep up with his more robust friend, and this rivalry made the backyard games a battleground on more than one occasion. The only reason I was allowed to join in, I suspect, was because they needed the extra team members. I tried to glamorise my role by taking on the persona of my cricketing hero Richie Benaud. I wasn't afraid to face a hard ball, and how I survived with my teeth intact is remarkable. Dan didn't. One of his pearly-white front teeth was snapped in half during a match, much to the dismay of our mother, who valued our dental health above all else because her own teeth had decayed at an early age.

In our teens our father somehow managed to scrape together enough money to buy a small yacht – I think it coincided with the death of his mother in Melbourne. In spite of her external poverty, his mother had been secretly prudent and managed to leave a legacy that allowed Dad to buy us some new household furniture, a gracious Spode dinner set and a boat called 'Sparkle'. It was a 24-foot sloop with a timber hull and elegant lines, and for a few years it made a huge difference to our family atmosphere and unity. Until then our lives had been bleak at the weekends, with our parents engrossed mostly in hitting the bottle and fighting. The boat gave us a new focus – it had to be maintained. With the encouragement of our older brother, Jon, Dad joined the Sydney Amateur Yacht Club and we entered into the Saturday afternoon racing calendar.

So we gave up swimming on Saturday afternoons and took up sailing. I loved it. For years Jon had been a crew member on a larger yacht, 'Cherub', owned by the feisty *Sun* newspaper yachting editor Lou D'Alpuget. He was an exacting but peerless skipper and Jon had learned well the tricks and techniques of Saturday racing. He passed them on to us and we enjoyed a degree of success during the three years we raced competitively. Because of my size and agility I was nominated for'ard hand and became adept at setting large spinnakers, but I was also expected to perform the female tasks: making tea and coffee below during the race, then breaking out the cold beers and rum once we were over the finishing line. It was a lot of fun, and a much needed diversion from the grimmer aspects of our daily life at home.

The summers of my adulthood were very different, mostly revolving around my passion for gardening and the sporting demands of my children. We lived a long way from the coast so the opportunities for swimming and sailing were rare. I was often asked if I missed the ocean and the beaches I grew up with, but I didn't. I have always felt more comfortable in the countryside. We bushwalked in the Mountains a lot, heading for the dramatic scenery of Wentworth Falls and Katoomba Cascades. We also had a favourite picnic spot in the Megalong Valley, where we would climb a fence into private farmland. The river there had created the most cooling summer pool for swimming. And unlike Balmoral, there were no sharks.

In France, the summer pastimes are rural and quite different from any I have experienced in Australia. Apart from the 'fêtes' – the village weekend celebrations that involve a lot of eating and drinking and dancing in the village square – the summers are punctuated by a non-stop round of markets or sales that specialise in second-hand goods, from the stylish brocantes (antique fairs) and salons des livres (antiquarian book markets), to the more downmarket vide greniers (attic clearances) and trocs (which translates literally as a 'swap' or 'exchange' gathering but in truth is more of a car boot sale). In my first year in France, shopping at these markets was a waste of time as I couldn't imagine lugging treasures back to Australia. But now that we have a house they have become a compulsive part of summer life. Even though you arrive knowing that the goods on sale will either be too extravagantly expensive or total rubbish, you can't resist going just in case there is a bargain to be found.

Generally I find the brocantes out of our price range except for small items such as occasional bits of china or those traditional crystal salt and pepper servers. The fabulous walnut and oak armoires and classic French beds cost thousands of euros, and anyway our house is too small to accommodate them – they would look out of place and would dwarf our rooms, which have comparatively low ceilings. I am aware that Australian antique dealers travel to France every summer just to collect charming pieces to fill a container and send back to the smart shops that specialise in 'genuine French antiques'. But while I appreciate that compared to the prices charged for similar items back home these are probably cheap, I simply don't know enough about it to get involved in seriously hunting down treasures. I suppose that says something about me: back in Australia I am not driven to auctions or antique fairs to gather objects for my home, so it's not surprising that here I have adopted a similar attitude. A few comfortable chairs, a good bed and some bits and pieces of dubious quality are quite enough to satisfy my needs and my tastes.

David, never a keen shopper at the best of times, is quickly bored by these non-food markets and can only see the junk that's on offer, not the possibility of something useful or beautiful hidden beneath the detritus. But during this hot summer he does develop a bit of a passion – more for the game of bargaining down the prices with the stallholders than for the actual items themselves. One Saturday while driving to Cahors we pass through Goujounac, where a vide grenier is under way. There are only about twenty-five stalls, mostly in the new 'halle', and I insist we stop the car and get out to browse.

'Ten minutes, that's all,' says David, squeezing the Peugeot into a space that's rather too small.

I systematically go from stall to stall, stooping to look at folded lengths of linen and lace in old cardboard boxes and rummaging through the shoeboxes overflowing with dusty costume jewellery. An old suitcase catches my eye because it is filled with grubby china that has a pretty design – a matching set in pink and yellow with a gold edging. I stop for a closer look. When I turn the plates over I see the 'Limoges' stamp on the back – an indication that the china has been made in the town to our north that has long been famous for its exquisite china. The stallholder shows me a second box, also full of the matching set, which has the letters 'TLB' and an emblem of a rooster also stamped on the underside. A quick calculation tells me there are more than sixty pieces, including plates of two sizes, bowls and some delightful serving platters, dishes and jardinieres.

The stallholder wants 150 euros and I call David over for a

look. He agrees that it's beautiful china but thinks the price too high and begins to negotiate in his almost non-existent French, ending up at a figure of 98 euros the lot. It's in the boot of the car before I can blink an eye. Then I spot a set of three orange Le Creusot saucepans (from the seventies obviously) in very good condition and this time they only want 15 euros – the new ones cost a small fortune, even here in France. But David still wants to haggle, and in the end he gets them for 12 euros. A genuine bargain. Normally I hate shopping with David. It makes me nervous the way he hovers impatiently and frowns whenever I pick up something to examine it more closely. But here in France I can see that we could easily get hooked on hunting for bargains as a team.

Normally these markets are crammed with foreign holiday-makers also looking for bargains, but this year the numbers seem to be down a little and this makes it easier for haggling. The heat has probably driven people indoors and discouraged them from making the effort to go out shopping. The markets are generally held out in the open in village squares, with the goods arranged on tables or spread out on the ground. I love the old garden tools that have been rescued from the back of derelict stone barns, and I'm always on the look-out for pastis bottles, which I am starting to collect. Pastis is the anise-flavoured aperitif so loved in the rural regions of France. Poured from the bottle it is a pale yellow liquid, then water is added to the glass and it turns a milky white. The water bottles, always labelled with the brand name, come in different shapes and sizes, and there are also porcelain water jugs that a lot of people like to collect and display on their bars.

The costume and heirloom jewellery at the markets is also

worth looking at. I have a friend in Australia who makes interesting individual pieces of jewellery, many in art deco style, and she has given me a budget and asked me to search for unusual beads and chains and buckles and clasps that she may be able to adapt for her work. I really have no idea what I am looking for, but it makes the searching more fun as I target every stall with old baskets and boxes of discarded junky jewellery. I also find various bits I like for myself – chunky silver earrings in the shape of a pussycat's face and brightly coloured necklaces that demonstrate that for very little money you can be adorned with gaudy cast-offs that are unique. Perhaps not to everyone's taste, but I love them.

I have also observed that for every interesting or worthwhile treasure for sale there are at least a hundred ugly artefacts – the tables are groaning with French bad taste, which may seem like a contradiction in terms but is in fact the truth. The French seem to have the best and worst of taste, and I never cease to be amazed at the hideous items that are seriously on display with a price tag attached. Some of my favourites revolve around the local rural passion for hunting. There are caps with a wild boar's head (sanglier) embroidered into the brim and dainty deer antlers that have been transformed into hat racks or hooks for keys. Deer feet are also used as handles for salad servers, and there are stuffed heads of various dead animals that have been mounted for display. Usually old and mouldy and always grotesque.

Clocks and lamps are another case in point. There is virtually no object that cannot be converted into a useful wall clock or tasteless lamp, including wooden clogs, plates, bottles, shells and jugs. I make the mistake of expressing my delight at the bizarre nature of some of the items on sale and my friends take the opportunity to buy me hideous gifts they stumble across at vide greniers or trocs. My friends Tony and Terry ceremoniously present me with a large blue porcelain clock that is a representation of a naked man clubbing a cougar to death. All he is wearing is a wispy loin cloth, and the clock face is somehow incorporated into this unappealing sculpture. I position it on top of the fridge.

Next Jan buys me a telephone cover made from dusty mustard velvet and glittering gold braid. Every part of the telephone is covered, including the handset, and there's a cute circular flap to lift when one needs to dial the number. It takes pride of place on the sideboard. Philippe discovers a 1960s vibrator, thinly disguised as a 'personal massager', with all sorts of telling line drawings and instructions in the booklet, which appears to have remained untouched all these years. An unappreciated gift, I expect. I plug it in to try out some of the vibrating attachments but am nearly electrocuted for my trouble as the French system has changed since this handy appliance was manufactured and now runs on a much higher voltage. I thank Philippe for his thoughtfulness.

So it goes on, until we decide to turn the game into a competition of sorts. Over one dinner, after several bottles of wine, we decide to launch an 'Exposition de Merde' or 'Exposition des Exquisites' – both names are bandied about, but a final decision is never made. At any rate, an exhibition of items collected at various vide greniers and trocs during the summer months. There is only one rule: the item must cost five euros or less. The idea is that we each collect an item and at the end of the summer we hold an exhibition and pronounce a winner.

We have not thought ahead to the fine detail – where to have the exhibition and what will happen to all the goodies afterwards. It just means that whenever one of us goes to a second-hand market there is a specific goal: looking for something truly hideous to outdo the competition. And trying not to let any of the others in the competition see what you have found – we all live in the same area and go to the same markets. It gives the summer a focus. It becomes a game: getting to the market first to blitz the stalls before anyone else. Sneaking off with the item of ghastly kitsch and hiding it away for the end-of-season competition.

26

If Miriam had survived the three-week holiday in France without pining for her children, they are certainly making her pay for it now. Back into the stride of her daily routine with four small boys, she barely has time to bounce back from her jetlag when things start to go awry. Rick returns to work, leaving early, and the two older boys continue the school term. One morning the youngest, two-year-old Augustus (known as Gus) is found crying helplessly in his cot, not greeting the day with his customary loud laughter and boisterous good humour. Miriam clucks over him and lifts him out. He won't go onto the floor and can't seem to walk. He has a slight fever and complains of a sore abdomen. She bundles him into the car and takes the two big boys to school, continuing on to hospital outpatients with Gus and his older brother Theo.

After an interminable wait, during which Gus whimpers in pain, they see a doctor and Gus is quickly admitted to the children's ward with suspected septic arthritis. All Miriam's children are recovering from colds. Septic arthritis is a rare opportunistic infection, like bronchitis, which can follow a childhood cold or flu. It manifests as a pool of infection in the hip joint and the child experiences intense pain, fever and inability to walk. The treatment is a massive dose of antibiotics and constant monitoring to ensure that the infection subsides.

Having just returned to work after Miriam's three-week absence, Rick has to request compassionate leave to look after the three older boys while Miriam keeps a vigil at Gus's hospital bedside. They swap shifts in the evening after dinner. Rick comes into the hospital while Miriam goes home and spends the night with the big children, swapping back in the morning. Theo goes to pre-school the following day so Rick is able to work, at least from 9 a.m. until school finishes at 3 p.m.

They are told that if Gus's infection doesn't resolve he will have to be transferred to a larger hospital in nearby Orange for monitoring and possibly surgery. They will make an opening into the hip socket and drain away any infected material.

On the second day, with the older children in school and pre-school, Miriam waits for the verdict of the visiting paediatrician. He examines Gus closely and says he feels it would be wise for him to transfer to Orange. His temperature hasn't dropped enough to indicate that the infection is clearing. Miram is about to phone Rick and tell him that he will have to look after the other children while she travels by ambulance the 45 minutes to Orange with Gus when the phone rings in the children's ward. It's for Miriam. Eamonn, the eldest, is in the sick bay at school and needs to be collected. For the first time ever, Miriam leaves Gus alone in the hospital and makes the dash to Eamonn's school, feeling somewhat irritated at his appalling timing. It's probably just a tummy upset.

She brings Eamonn back to the hospital and sticks him on a chair in the corner while she continues to make arrangements with the paediatrician for Gus's imminent transfer. The doctor glances over in Eamonn's direction.

'What's his problem?' he enquires in a distracted way.

'Goodness knows,' says Miriam. 'Probably sick of school, or not getting enough attention.'

'I'll take a quick look at him.'

Within ten minutes, Eamonn has been admitted into the hospital with acute appendicitis.

'He's really quite a sick little boy,' the doctor tells Miriam. 'We'll have to operate this afternoon.'

So Rick catches the ambulance to Orange with Gus while Miriam stays by Eamonn's bedside, holding his hand as he is prepared for surgery. Both boys have their operations within hours of each other, and friends look after Sam and Theo, who seem quite jolly in the face of all the excitement.

That day I've been trying to call Miriam at home in Bathurst, unaware of the unfolding events. I can't understand why nobody is at home – not in the morning nor again in the evening. I keep calling, then eventually phone Ethan to see if he knows where they all are.

'Don't you know what's happened, Mum?' he says. Then regales me with the unbelievable saga.

It's moments like this that I regret being such an absent grandmother. Of course they cope without me, but I feel terrible that I haven't been there to help and lend support.

Both boys make a rapid recovery but Miriam feels totally drained by the experience. As though her therapeutic three weeks in France have been entirely expunged. At least she knows she's back home.

Two weeks later Eamonn goes back to see the paediatrician for a post-operative examination and he gives Miriam the results of the tests done on the contents of Eamonn's abdominal cavity at the time of surgery. His appendix had actually ruptured, and if he had been left much longer he could have been a very sick little boy indeed. In fact, he could easily have died. Miriam is shocked to realise how easy it is to overlook symptoms of childhood illness. Eamonn had left for school that morning seeming quite cheerful. By eight in the evening he was on the operating table. It's a frightening thought.

27

In Paris the workforce is getting ready to exit for annual August holidays. The schools, the government, the bureaucracy and most of the private sector take their holidays at the same time, and because it is the hottest month of the year most people head for the country or the coast. This year it's much hotter than usual and very few French homes, even in Paris, have air-conditioning. The heat rises off the road and inside buildings those living on the second, third and fourth floor apartments are experiencing heat like never before. A lot of elderly French people live alone rather than with their families. When the annual holiday exodus occurs, they are left to fend for themselves without children or grandchildren nearby to help out if there is a problem. Most of them live in old apartment blocks and very few have gardens or places where they can find shade to escape from the heat. The younger couples drive out of the city with their children, leaving the old people behind. Doctors leave, emergency services people leave, and hospitals are run with a skeleton staff. It's a recipe for disaster.

The farmers in and around the village talk about little else than the heatwave. It's been a catastrophe for their maize and sunflower crops, which are literally baking in the fields. In a normal summer the heads of corn would be plumping up by now, but instead they are stunted and withered. The heads of sunflowers, usually brilliant yellow and packed with shiny black seeds, have collapsed because the stems have been weakened by extreme heat and lack of water. They hang dismally, waiting for the farmers to rip them from the ground unharvested so that at very least what remains can be turned into silage. Nobody can remember such widespread loss of crops, and there are grave fears for the grape vines which, unlike in Australia, are rarely irrigated. The annual rainfall and temperatures are so reliable that irrigation is not considered necessary.

In spite of the heatwave, the tourist season appears as busy as ever and people are crowding to the Plan d'Eau every day, sitting in the shade of the oaks and dangling their legs into the cooling water. The Plan d'Eau is a large and very pretty manmade lake, edged with spreading trees, just around the corner from our house, and it's a haven for summer visitors. Christian from Le Relais opens a bar and outdoor restaurant here in the summer, serving cooling drinks and ice creams for the children and simple meals – moules frites (mussels and chips), grillade (mixed grill) and salads – for the adults. A local company hires out paddle boats and the lake is also used for fishing and swimming, although I don't fancy the idea of venturing into its murky shallows. It doesn't seem to faze the children, however, and there's lots of splashing and swimming out into the middle of the lake, which is much colder and therefore appealing on these long hot summer afternoons.

The lake feeds into a stream which snakes through the back of the village, running past neatly tended potager gardens bursting with summer vegetables and eventually under Claude's house – the old moulin (millhouse) – where it also feeds his ornamental pond. Sitting in the dappled light of the Plan d'Eau in the late afternoon is like stepping into a painting by Claude Monet, but this year I don't seem to get down there very often.

There's quite a different atmosphere to the three summers I have spent here before, and for us it is as though something more ominous, quite apart from the heat haze, is hanging in the air. I'm trying to write a novel and it seems to be going nowhere. I have written at least four separate opening chapters and lots of descriptive passages, yet when I read back over them I feel dissatisfied and frustrated with the result. It doesn't feel as though it's my voice that's telling the story. The writing seems stilted and forced. My heart sinks.

Since dropping Miriam off at the airport in Toulouse, David has become even more subdued and sullen. I admit I don't much have the heart for socialising either. I'm starting to feel rather frayed at the edges, and I suspect it's not just the heatwave.

We tend to wake early, have breakfast and do our overseas calls and emails. Then David heads off on his walk, and I either go shopping or make some attempts at continuing with my writing. We eat lunch together in the dark with the shutters pulled, and drink far too much rosé. An afternoon sleep leaves me feeling thick-headed, and in the evening I open the shutters hoping for a cooling breeze. We listen to music, have a light dinner and talk about nothing in particular.

Although we are not fighting the way we were when Miriam

was around, there's an uneasy feeling between us. A calm before the storm.

Having David around in his current frame of mind is certainly a dampener on my spirits. Usually I'm out and about, drinking in the bar, meeting people for dinner at the Plan d'Eau and having friends for dinner. This year we are both keeping a very low profile and the house has become like a prison. People don't knock on the front window any more asking me out for a drink, and the gay and carefree atmosphere I have enjoyed in the past has totally disappeared.

One evening, sitting together as it gets dark, I stand up to tidy the glasses away and get ready for bed. I'm not relishing yet another sweat-soaked sleepless night.

'Sit down,' says David. 'We need to talk.'

I am accustomed to David being intense, but nothing has prepared me for the bombshell he is about to drop.

'You have a new lover,' he says.

For me the ensuing conversation remains a blur to this day. What can I say? There's no point denying anything. David seems to know everything. Who the man is and when the affair began. David is a master of ambush. He knows when I am most vulnerable. Tired. End of the day. But I don't believe he deliberately chose this moment to lie in wait for me. He's obviously known for some little while, from way back early in Miriam's visit, and he's been stewing on it ever since. I don't think he could keep it to himself any more.

I am shattered. We are both shattered. All I can say is that I'm sorry. That I didn't intend to hurt him. I didn't want him to find out, ever. I'm sorry. I'm sorry.

David is much calmer and more resigned to the situation than

I ever could have imagined. He seems one step removed, as though it's happening to someone else, not him. In quiet conversation he says he always knew it was on the cards. It's the way these things go. He accepts it. He even understands it. I feel hollow and shocked and sick to the stomach. I am accustomed to David's immediate and passionate reactions to events that affect his life. It's how he has conducted himself during the thirty-three years of our cohabitation. He's such a black-and-white person. So definite in his beliefs. But now, twice over, he has reacted in a way that I couldn't have predicted. He's almost too calm and collected. I guess it's the shock of it all.

Remarkably, after the affair has been 'outed' the atmosphere in the house improves dramatically. As though the lid has been lifted off the pressure cooker. Suddenly we are talking again and making love passionately as an act of mutual comfort and reassurance. What has happened has given us both a big fright and we are doing our best to claw our way back together. All our life as partners has been punctuated by long separations followed by intense sexual reunions. And sex has always been used as a way of healing rifts whenever we have had serious arguments. Now we need it more than ever.

David is determined to have a conversation with my lover. I am terrified by the prospect. What can be gained? He claims that his knowledge of the affair was nothing more than a gradual realisation. Putting pieces together in a jigsaw to arrive at a conclusion. But I suspect he's been tipped off by one of the gossips, and he admits that he has already discussed the matter with some of our mutual friends, who have confirmed that there have been rumours around for quite some time. Nobody, it seems, was prepared to confirm these rumours but they were virulent enough to have had a deadly impact.

David only has a few weeks left in France. Before we left Australia, it had been agreed that he would spend a couple of months with me after the Cannes festival then leave me to work on my novel before the arrival of the walking tour group in September. At the time he expressed concern that I was 'trying to get rid of him' but I was adamant that I simply wanted some time to myself between his visit and the start of the tour, which always involves a lot of hard work. A little bit of down time. Some space to just do my own thing.

Now he is convinced that I planned the whole thing from the start. To allow him to come and stay for a while and then banish him back to Australia so that I can continue my affair. It sounds plausible from his point of view, but I try to convince him that none of this was ever planned or premeditated. It just evolved.

So David visits the home of my lover to confront him. My lover is prepared for this encounter, as we've had time for a brief conversation about the fact that our relationship has been discovered. It is apparently a calm and civilised meeting between the two men. Afterwards David tries to tell me the detail of their discussion but I refuse to listen. I am so mortified by the whole thing that I simply don't want to hear what has transpired. I have spent my life dodging confrontation, and even though he assures me there were no heated words or crossing of swords, the very thought of the conversation fills me with dismay. I realise of course that I have created the situation in which I now find myself, but I can't deal with the consequences. I know that even if I wanted to pick up the threads of my relationship with my lover, it is now impossible. And that, in itself, is a good thing.

David's way of handling the whole scenario is uncharacteristic. Most husbands would have reacted with immediate rage. Shouted, screamed, ranted, raved and then probably walked out the door. The marriage would have been over. Full stop. It's possible that one affair in thirty years can be tolerated. But two affairs in two years is unendurable. Yet he appears to be taking it all in his stride. He is affectionate towards me, we talk a lot and we make love more often than usual. However, he's drinking the local wine to excess. David is normally a moderate drinker. He's also now chain-smoking roll-your-own black Gauloise tobacco and is beginning to look raddled. The combination of the unabated heat, the stress, the drinking and the smoking are taking their toll. On both of us.

We are invited to, and agree now to attend, several summer parties as people try to counteract the heatwave by socialising as a diversion. David is concerned about the rumour mill and I reassure him that in France nobody much cares about these things. That we must tough it out and act as though nothing untoward has been happening. It's not easy. A couple of times we find ourselves at large gatherings where my lover is also in attendance. David and he always have a polite chat and outwardly there are no signs of the turmoil that is simmering away under the surface. I am so relieved that things haven't escalated into a giant uproar. We are all in our own way testing the water and it's an artificial attempt at normality. I have no idea who's talked to whom or what anybody knows. It's just a matter of keeping up appearances. Putting on a brave face.

One night, after a long, long lunch and a hot and breathless afternoon during which we have failed to sleep, we relax in our pretty sitting room and talk late into the night. On one hand,

David seems very pragmatic about the whole thing, but he wants to talk about the future. My intentions. I say, as I have said over and over these past two years, that the last thing I want is for our marriage to end. That I love him and that our family is more important to me than anything in the world. He knows that to be true.

But I cannot promise that this will never happen again. I must be honest here. I know that I am in a very highly charged emotional state and that to guarantee that I will just stop now, settle down and go back to being the wife I was before all this happened would be totally unrealistic. I want to leave things open-ended. Dangling.

'I'll get through this phase,' I say to try and assuage his doubts. 'Just give me time until I get whatever it is that's troubling me out of my system.'

His final words on the 'Australian Story' documentary return to me over and over. Like a mantra:

'I'm not a forgiving person but I could forgive Mary Moody anything. I love her that much.'

I have convinced myself that this is the crux of the matter. I am going through a rocky period because of my age, because of the difficulties of our long-term relationship and because of my unsettled sexuality. But I will recover my senses and everything will work out okay in the long run.

I really am kidding myself.

As a very different summer diversion, I find myself getting involved in a local cricket match to be played at the nearby village of Montcléra. There are two teams of mostly English expats, with the odd Australian and New Zealander thrown in where needed. I am told they are desperate for more players and I rashly volunteer myself and am quite startled when they take me up on my offer. I haven't played cricket for forty years, but I feel certain it will be a good-natured match and only hope the bowlers are either inept or modify the speed of their balls in my direction.

I try to convince David he should also play. He played competition cricket as a kid in New Zealand, but like me hasn't played for decades, except on the beach with a tennis ball during family summer holidays. He's quite fit from the past few years of constant exercising but really doesn't want to pull on a pair of cricket pads. I don't blame him really, because by now I'm wishing I had kept my big mouth shut.

I nervously go along for a practice session a few days prior to the match. I am the only woman in either team, and while a lot of the blokes are middle-aged and not especially fit, there are also several keen young male players, which is slightly unsettling. We all have a turn at batting and I manage to hit the ball first swing, unlike a lot of the others. I can't hit it very hard or very far, but at least I can hit it. I decline bowling – I have never been good at this and know I will do the typical female thing of chucking the ball lamely in the direction of the wicket. It will be far too embarrassing. But I am quite quick off the mark fielding, stopping the ball with my foot rather than catching it. I have small, finely boned hands.

On the day of the match we set off early with a picnic packed with cold quiche, salad, wine, cheese and crusty bread. David is dressed for the occasion in white jacket and Panama hat. We take chairs and cushions and our spirits are quite high. Within minutes of arriving he is roped reluctantly into being one of the scorers in tandem with one of the wives – an outrageous English-woman called Fanny whose Irish husband is on the opposite team. They set up under an umbrella and David struggles to remember the scoring rules from all those years ago. He's now sixty-four and the last time he scored a match he would have been sixteen. It comes back gradually over the day.

Montcléra is a picture postcard village about ten minutes up the road from Frayssinet. It has a feudal feel to it, with modest stone cottages clustered around an imposing château that some locals describe as being 'a little bit Walt Disney' because of its rounded turrets with pointy slate roofs. The château is owned by a French family from Paris and not foreigners – which makes the village even more unusual these days – and every year they host an art exhibition in their palatial barn. This weekend there is a village fête with various musical events and a feast cooked by the local women. The plan is for members of both cricket teams to come back in the evening for the meal if we are still capable of walking after a day of vigorous exercise.

The oval we are playing on is a local soccer field with woodlands all around and a gentle slope where the spectators set up with blankets and umbrellas. The weather is hot, but mercifully not quite as hot as the preceding few weeks, and there's even a little cloud around to bring relief to those who will be fielding. I notice that there are virtually no French people around – this is very much a gathering of expats and their families and friends who are down holidaying for the summer.

We win the toss and go in to bat. I am listed as the last in to bat, for obvious reasons. That means I will spend the morning watching, remembering some of the rules I have long forgotten, and cheering our team on to score. I have managed to rope in an extra player, the grandson of an Australian friend who is renting Claude's barn for the summer with various members of her family. He's a tall strapping lad who looks to be in his late teens but is only fourteen. He is co-opted onto the other team, who are thrilled to have the full complement. He's a very keen player and bowls admirably. I wish he was on our team instead.

During the morning my French friend Lucienne's daughter Ann, on holiday from Paris, arrives at the field. I spend some time trying to explain the rules of the game to her, but I can see she's entirely baffled and bemused.

'What is everyone doing now?' she asks as the fielders change position at the end of each over. I try to describe the strategies but she still looks totally bemused. I guess you have to be born and brought up with cricket to make sense of it all.

People sit in small happy groups and cheer loudly if a couple of runs are made or if one of our batsmen is bowled out. David seems to be really enjoying himself and it's the first time I've seen him look relaxed and comfortable since he arrived. It could be that most of these people are new to him – not our usual circle of friends – so he feels somehow distanced from the reality of what has happened. I sit on a rug near the table where he and Fanny are keeping score and it feels good to be here. The fact that we are playing a very English game on a foreign field doesn't seem to matter. The day is hot yet not stifling, cakes and sandwiches and hot tea are being passed around, and somehow the world seems okay.

The decision is made for our team to retire from batting at lunchtime regardless of whether all the players have been bowled. I'm the last player to go out, looking rather awkward in oversize pads and gloves. I face the bowler and try not to be intimidated. I hope they will lob me a few gentle balls and not try to massacre me.

The first bowler is kind. I hit the ball wildly but not very far several times, then finally manage a decent whack and score a couple of runs. I don't care much after that. Some of the blokes were out for a duck, so as long as I can hold the fort until lunchtime I will feel I have more than done my bit.

I play conservatively and realise that some of the opposite team players on the field are sending me up. Sledging me, but in a humorous rather than a malicious fashion. They sing out that they can see my knickers through my white pants. I do my best to ignore them. David is amazed at the way I'm hanging in. I am just determined not to get out. Lunch is called and we have scored 183 runs. The batswoman not out for three. I am hot from standing out in the midday sun with all the mad dogs and Englishmen and can't wait for a cold drink.

Our team has a little meeting before we settle down to our picnic and I put forward a strategy. 'If we can get them drunk on wine during the lunch break they will crumble,' I suggest.

I have several bottles of chilled rosé in our esky and I wander through the opposition team topping up their glasses while sticking to water myself. They are hot and frazzled from standing out on the field all morning. Their first batsman takes a bottle of red wine out to the stumps and swigs from it before facing the first ball. I know we've got them. We will prevail.

My young friend, the fourteen-year-old, plays brilliantly and lifts the score for his team. He obviously isn't swigging wine like the rest of them. The language on the field gets pretty rough as the afternoon wears on. I come in for a lot of flak but I remain buoyant. In the end we win by just three runs. The three runs I got, I like to kid myself.

After the match, the wives produce high tea under the shade of some nearby oak trees. There are cucumber sandwiches and cream cakes and tea or coffee, though most of the men have opted for cold beer. We have about an hour left to go home, shower and change then come back for the village fête. We book a table and gather up our picnic baskets.

The evening is balmy and most of the cricket players have opted for staying and drinking beer under the oak trees rather than going home to clean up. They look a motley bunch as we take our seats at the long trestle tables for the meal to be served. It's a well-organised event – unlike some fêtes where the food doesn't appear until late in the evening, sometimes even midnight. We have good chicken soup with bread and an entrée of local wild boar terrine followed by spit-roasted lamb and potatoes with a chestnut sauce. There is cheese – my favourite fromage de chèvre (goat's cheese) – and a rich apple tart for dessert. The wine flows steadily, although after the main course we are expected to pay for extra bottles – the tariff for the meal is about 15 euros and includes everything, but the French tend to stop drinking once the meal has finished. It's the foreign holidaymakers who like to swill on into the night.

The best part of the day is when a group of local women, all well into their seventies and eighties, perform a series of comedy sketches in the ancient regional language, Occitan, which is still spoken here but only by the older generation. It's amusing to see the French in the audience, who are just as out of their depth as we are because they can't follow the dialogue. Fortunately the sketches are very visual, almost slapstick, and everyone roars their approval.

It's days like this that remind me why I love it here so much. I only wish that a little of the pleasure of it might rub off on David.

30

In many ways a crisis in a marriage is a great way to shake things up. To open up wide-ranging discussion and to face some of the demons of our past life. When David and I talk about everything we have been through we have to be careful not to go over and over and over the same issues because eventually we'd find ourselves just talking in circles and getting nowhere. But our hope is that through all this pain a clearer picture has emerged of who we really are. There's no time now for anything but total honesty, and some of our conversations are quite brutal as we confront each other and try to make a way ahead.

David says he doesn't recognise me any more. That I am simply not the woman he thought he was living with for all those years. He's pretty straightforward in admitting that he preferred the old me. But that's only natural. The old me was a known quantity. Steady, reliable, faithful, loyal and loving. The mother of his children. The grandmother of his grandchildren. His partner, both in business and in life.

David has been forced to acknowledge some unpalatable home truths about himself and about our relationship. He looks back at the years when our children were growing up, when he was so often absent because of his career. He admits now that he was unaware of how unhappy I was with that situation. It's partly my fault. I should have been more forceful and insistent. But David is a very stubborn man. Inflexible. Almost impossible to shift once he has determined that things have to be done in a certain way. Single-minded. Blinkered. Intractable.

Not that I am without myriad faults. I am impulsive, impatient and wilful. A spendthrift who is irresponsibly generous when we can least afford it. I overcommit myself and I am constantly trying to accomplish more in a day than is humanly possible. I rush at things like a bull at a gate. I often don't think things through clearly, preferring to leap into action rather than pause for reflection. If something is worrying me, I do my best to ignore it. Hope that it will simply go away. I hide bills I don't want to pay and 'forget' to return phone calls if I know I have to let someone down. I become irrationally emotional about political and social injustice. I feel things too deeply and allow myself to be badly hurt by events that are out of my control. I don't necessarily make that vital connection between cause and effect.

David has therefore been a good balance for me. I try to help lighten him up and he tries to help rein me in a little. My flamboyance is tempered by his more staid perspective. His ability to manage finances has saved us from bankruptcy on more than one occasion. If left to me, we would be perpetually penniless. Opposites attract, or so they say. Perhaps that's why we have remained together for so long.

During our lengthy conversations I try to give him an

understanding of just how much I have changed. Why I must have this time and space to sort out who I am and where I am going. As a way of further illustrating how the last few years have been just as harrowing for me as they have been for him, I tell him about the attack. The night the Englishman hid in the house and then tried to rape me.

He sits in his chair and eyeballs me with a look of utter horror on his face. 'Why didn't you tell me about this before?' he asks. 'How could you not phone me when it happened? You told other people. You didn't tell me. You didn't tell me.'

I lamely give my reasons.

'I thought you would feel helpless being so far away. I didn't want to worry or upset you. I thought you'd think I was incapable of looking after myself. I thought it would be better if I just dealt with it myself and didn't burden you.'

'You didn't tell me. You didn't tell me.'

Not one thing that has happened until now has disturbed David as much as this. Immediately I wish I hadn't told him. He is distraught. Angry with me, really angry for the first time.

'Don't you see,' he shouts at me. 'This means you think so little of me and so little of our relationship that you didn't even tell me that you had been viciously sexually assaulted. You hid from me something that was fundamental to the validity of our relationship. I can't believe you didn't tell me.'

I suppose this means I just don't understand men and the workings of their minds. I try to fathom why David has been so deeply upset by this latest revelation. Surely my infidelities have been more damaging to the trust in our relationship than the fact that I protected him from knowing something that would cause him pain.

I seem to be making a total mess of my entire life. I have no one to blame but myself.

Just when things between us are as bad as they could possibly be we get a phone call from Australia, from our son Ethan who normally doesn't phone because of the cost. He and Lynne are living on a pretty tight budget. My first reaction is to imagine there's a problem, perhaps with little Isabella, so I am immediately anxious. But Ethan sounds bright and bubbly and asks lots of questions about our friends and neighbours in the village, where they lived for six months when Lynne was pregnant. He then tells us the real reason for the call.

'I have some exciting news,' he says. 'Lynne's pregnant. We're having another baby.'

The reaction he gets from me is so emotional that I simply can't speak because I'm overcome. I have to hand the phone over to David to finish the conversation. Nothing in the world could have made us happier than this. We have been frightened that Ethan and Lynne would not be brave enough to attempt having another child, given the severity of Isabella's condition. I feared that they would never experience the joy of being the parents of a healthy, problem-free child. A child who sits up at six months and walks at twelve months and is talking non-stop by the age of two. Although Isabella's condition is undoubtedly genetic, the thought of the new baby being affected isn't an issue for us, or for them either, it seems. The likelihood of two children with the same rare set of symptoms is highly, highly unlikely.

An hour after the call I am still very teary. It has brought me back to earth with a big jolt because it's so obvious to me that this is far, far more important than any of the argy-bargy that's been going on between David and me. Our troubles are trivial compared to those confronting Ethan and Lynne and their children. It puts the whole thing into perspective and serves to remind me that my family is, after all, the most precious thing in my life.

31

 I drive David to Toulouse to catch his plane back to Australia. He's travelling on a cheap business class ticket, which means he has a four-day stopover in Hong Kong, something he's really not looking forward to. He is subdued and melancholy. I am feeling totally drained by the last few weeks and quite honestly will be pleased when he's gone, so I can have some time on my own to mentally process everything that has happened. If I was confused about my life before the last two months, I am now even more unsettled and uncertain.

We are both quite subdued on the journey south, talking more about the effects of the heatwave on the crops and woods in this region than about our ongoing marital problems. The fields that adjoin the motorway are filled with burnt and frizzled stems of maize and sunflowers. The vineyards don't seem to have suffered as much damage, but the surrounding hillsides are very telling, dotted with dead and dying oak and chestnut trees all through the woods. A lot of the vegetation here, as in Australia, has grown naturally on very shallow, rocky ground. Over the summer the roots have remained dry for so long that the trees themselves have started to die. It's the first time we have ever observed the northern hemisphere looking like Australia in the summer, faded and dry.

After his bags have been checked in, David turns to hug and kiss me good-bye. 'I guess you'll be glad to see the back of me,' he says with a slight smile.

I deny it, of course, but he knows me well enough to know the truth. I need a break from him and from our deeply troubled relationship.

In the car driving back from the airport to Frayssinet, I put my foot flat to the boards. David always cautions me to drive the old Peugeot slowly. He believes it isn't safely capable of more than 100 kmh. But it's a lively little car and easily reaches 140 kmh on the motorway. I open the sunroof and inhale a sense of freedom and release. And relief.

This isn't right. I should be feeling sad that David is leaving. But I feel elated that I don't have to grapple with the difficulties any more. They haven't disappeared, of course, they have just moved out of sight for a little while.

I throw myself back into the party scene and start getting organised for the walking tour. The book isn't making much progress. I seem to be stuck mid-sentence. It's symptomatic of my entire life. Going nowhere.

My lover is away visiting friends in southern France and this allows me some space to do a little clear thinking. I have had no conversation with him since the day he and David met and talked, and I am concerned that he must have found the entire episode gruelling. I hope we can now revert to our former relationship – that of just being friends. It would certainly take the pressure off us both.

I hear not a word from David for the four days he is in transit. Normally he would call from Hong Kong every day for a chat, but this time there is complete silence. On the fifth day, he phones to say he has arrived back at the farm to total catastrophe. It's freezing cold at Yetholme. Snowing. A pipe linked to the hot water service in the attic has frozen and then burst, flooding the kitchen, bathroom, linen cupboard and one of the bedrooms. Fortunately our neighbour Robert Porter found the disaster within hours of it happening, but even so the water damage is extensive. Robert had been up to the house in the early morning checking the animals and at that stage everything seemed to be in order. For some reason he popped back in just before lunchtime, knowing that David would be arriving in the late afternoon. In the intervening period thousands of litres of water had cascaded into the house. He managed to turn off the water and mop up just before David came up the drive. It's a deeply depressing, distressing homecoming.

To add to the gloom, David discovers that rats have made a nest in our bedroom and dressing room. There are rat droppings everywhere and a huge amount of damage to our clothing. His best suit has been gnawed at the shoulder. And my new hat. David is very careful with his clothes. He looks after them and they last for years and years. He is horrified at the extent of the damage.

I can just imagine how terrible he is feeling having to deal with all of this on his own, especially after having been through such an emotionally draining couple of months. Coming from the intense heat of that French summer to grey skies, minus five degrees and a house that has been flooded and invaded by vermin.

If I had half a heart I'd jump on the next plane home to help him. But I don't.

32

 By mid-August the heatwave in France has reached a terrifying climax. August 12 is considered the deadliest day, with literally thousands of reported deaths all over the country. More than half of the casualties are elderly patients in nursing homes. The homes and aged-care hostels are critically short of staff because so many people are on annual leave. Those that remain simply can't keep on top of the problem. People are dying of heat exhaustion, heat stroke and dehydration. The hospitals can't cope, they are overflowing and are also gravely understaffed. The morgues can't cope with the sheer volume of bodies. Refrigerated trucks are hired to store cadavers and makeshift morgues are set up in cool rooms all over Paris. At one point more than three hundred bodies remain unclaimed. Families on holiday simply aren't aware that their elderly relatives have perished.

In August alone 56,000 people die, which is 15,000 more than usual at this time of year. Most of them are considered to be heat-related deaths.

There are immediate political repercussions. Ministers and their staff start returning to Paris. There are press releases and statements denying that the heatwave could have been predicted and therefore emergency procedures put in place. The Director General of Health resigns and the American media use the situation to have a swing at the French, claiming that the disaster is a result of stupidity because the French have failed to adopt air-conditioning as a way of life in the same way people have done in the United States. This is all happening at the same time that the French and Americans are at loggerheads over the plans to invade Iraq, so the heatwave has left the French wide open for international criticism. The irony is that the French have what is considered to be the highest quality health care service in the world, but even that couldn't prevent the August catastrophe.

During the remainder of August I live in a hot and hazy cloud of muddled thoughts and ideas. I catch up with my ex-lover again when he returns from his holiday and he admits that he was indeed badly shaken by his encounter with David.

But I'm still ambivalent about what I want to do with the rest of my life. I love it here but I know that the experience of owning a French cottage has been totally spoiled for David. Probably forever. I am now yearning to go home to Australia, to the farm and to my family. I know that I don't want to give up my husband, my home, my family and my way of life for a romantic escapade. But the entire experience has left me addled. In so many ways, I really don't know who I am any more.

In an attempt to lift my flagging spirits, I throw a party to celebrate the end of the kitsch-buying season. It's the culmina-tion of our summer-long competition to see who can find the most frightful object at one of the antique markets, sticking strictly to a budget of 5 euros or less. After some discussion about where the exhibition is to be held, I decide I can somehow squeeze everyone into our little house – again spilling out into the courtyard.

Jan and I set the house up like a gallery exhibition, with plastic tables covered with white cloths. I ask everyone to drop off their exhibits the day before and we are amazed at the breadth of kitsch that people have managed to gather. We set up and number the objects, each with a card explaining the place of purchase and the price. The idea is that people arriving pick a number out of a hat and at the end of the evening, after the judging and announcement of winners, everyone will take home one item. Well, that's the plan, anyway.

The exhibits are truly horrific. Clocks decorated with seashells and ashtrays made in the shape of women's breasts and lamps that are ugly black ceramic hands holding flashing globes. Lots of sparkles and feathers and false deer feet. I order a pile of pizzas and serve chilled rosé by the pitcher. It's a highly amusing evening. The winner is a cruet set – salt, pepper and mustard bowl – in the shape of a toilet. The mustard is served from the toilet bowl with a wooden lid and small wooden spoon, the salt and pepper from two adjoining potties. It's quite the most awful thing I have ever seen.

At the end of the night people pour out the door laughing and happy, but I notice nobody is picking up their 'lucky door prize' as they leave. As I should have expected, I am abandoned with a room full of ghastly objets d'art. The whole exhibition ends up in boxes in the attic. I could now hold a vide grenier of my own if I wanted to.

My tour group arrives in September just as the heatwave

breaks. They are full of enthusiasm and can't wait for the two weeks of rambling around the beautiful Lot. I feel like a wrung-out dishcloth. Not just from surviving the heatwave, but from surviving my rollercoaster ride of a life. But they are a great bunch of people and their zest for discovering the region quickly infects me with new energy. This year the tour group is small, only eight people – again because the aftermath of the Bali bombings has made Australians rather reluctant tourists.

Jan and I go to their hotel just before they are due to get off the train from Paris and leave a basket of comforting goodies for their arrival: cheese and biscuits, bottled water, fruit and chocolates. Those who have made the long journey from Australia probably won't feel like going out for dinner on the first night, and a few supplies should keep them going.

The aim of the tour is to give people a really personal intro-duction to this part of France, so instead of just visiting the best-known touristy destinations we try to get off the beaten track and see the 'real' France that I have grown to love so much. We spend the mornings walking – sometimes through the woods, sometimes from one village to the next, sometimes along the banks of the winding River Lot and sometimes from a château to a vineyard. Our lunches are mostly informal picnics with a basket of local delicacies that have been packed up for us by Christiane in the village. There's something different every day and most of it is homemade in her kitchen. Terrines and pâtés and grilled chicken, cold roasted meats and salads. We try wines from different regions, mostly rosé and red, and finish with a delicious tart or gateau. In the afternoons we go sightseeing by bus.

There are so many places to visit in this region, from the prehistoric grottes (caves) at Gourdon to the ancient pilgrim

towns of Rocamadour and Puy l'Eveque. In the evenings it's time
to eat seriously, and we have selected some of the best traditional
restaurants we can find. Experience has taught us to vary the
menu, as people tend to get 'ducked out' after a week of stuffing
their faces with foie gras and confit du canard (preserved duck);
there's only so much goose fat a person can tolerate. So we try
to arrange set menus with lamb, fish or beef as an alternative.

Each group that comes to do the tour has a different dynamic,
depending on the personalities of the participants. This group
is loud and boisterous, with several hilarious people who have us
in fits of laughter all day long. The common thread is that they
just want to experience this part of the world and soak up as
much of the local colour and flavour as possible.

One of our favourite destinations is the Marqueyssac Gardens,
just inside the Dordogne. Set high on the edge of a steep hillside
overlooking the river, the garden is long and narrow and has two
distinct areas: a formal parterre with clipped box hedges, and
woodland which has winding paths and spectacular views. The
parterre is remarkable in that it was totally derelict until seven
years ago, with the hedges overgrown and indistinct with no
shape or form visible. With love and care it has been cut back
and restored to its former glory, and we just love rambling
through the sculptured hedges, looking out over the valley with
grand châteaux dotted around the landscape. It's breathtaking.

The small village of Les Arques, not fifteen minutes from
where I live, is also popular with the group. The village has
become an artists' centre because it was once home to the
famous Russian-born sculptor Ossip Zadkine, and several of the
larger buildings have been converted into lodgings where artists
can come and work for months at a time. In more recent years

the village has also become famous because of its restaurant, La Récréation, which serves imaginative non-traditional food and was the subject of a popular book, *You Can't See Paris From Here*, by Michael Sanders. We always have a dinner at this delightful place and the tour group finds it a pleasant change from the richer and heavier local cuisine. The signature dish at La Récréation is an entrée of lobster ravioli – I order it every time I visit because it is just so delicious.

During the tour I try to spend a quiet little time at the house every day, just to gather my thoughts and regain my energy for the following day. There's just so much to be done keeping the group busy, and moving them from town to town every four days certainly keeps me on my toes.

I speak to David almost daily and he certainly sounds a bit more cheerful. He has had the onerous task of taking every dripping wet sheet, towel and pillowcase from the linen cupboard and washing it. The weather is too cold and damp for line drying, so he has painstakingly put every item through the clothes dryer. He has been running electric heaters in the affected rooms and the linen cupboard in the hope of drying things out. The pest exterminator has been and the rats appear to have vacated or died. I guess, in a perverse sort of way, it has taken his mind off our troubles.

We talk about our problems but not in any great detail. I know he has been relying on the children a lot for moral support. Miriam in particular has been a tower of strength for both of us. She's very approachable and offers commonsense advice. I feel badly that the kids have to put up with our trials and tribulations. They have families and lives of their own and they don't need to be burdened with our marital problems at this stage of their lives. I keep telling David that I am looking forward to coming home and settling back into my real life. He doesn't sound very convinced but still manages to say 'I love you' at the end of every call.

One evening during the tour Miriam phones. She tells me that she and her brothers have been talking and they have something they need to communicate to me. Something serious, and I must listen.

'Look Mum,' she says. 'You've got to make up your mind. You just can't go on like this. It's killing Dad. It's driving him absolutely crazy. And we are the ones here having to deal with the consequences. None of us can stand to see him like this any more. He is so unhappy. You've just got to make up your mind.'

She's right. I know damn well she's right. I have to do something. I can't just let the situation go on and on with me wanting to stay married one moment then wanting to be a carefree single woman in France the next. But I am still uncertain about the course of action I should take. I wish somebody would wave a magic wand over my head and tell me which way to go.

33

David and I have discussed giving ourselves some time after I get back. I am due home at the beginning of October. Within days of returning I will be thrown into the publicity tour for *Last Tango*. The plan is that David will travel with me for the first week of the tour, starting at the Brisbane Writers' Festival and then to Sydney where I am booked to speak at a Dymocks/*Sydney Morning Herald* literary lunch at the Sheraton Hotel. It is all very exciting. But once the book launch and promotion are out of the way, we will have Christmas together with the whole family and then sit down in January or February and try to make some serious long-term decisions. I know that I will be able to think more clearly and rationally when I am back at the farm. Here in France everything seems like a blur, as though my vision is clouded.

Just as they always have been, our working lives are very separate and often diverse. While I am leading the tour group through the backblocks of France, David is having meetings for a film project that he has been developing for some time. The meetings are productive and the project seems to be moving forward, which he finds not only encouraging but also a relief. The film industry has been going through a downturn for several years, and getting projects up and running has become increasingly difficult and frustrating. But this project must be going along extremely well, because when he phones he sounds energised and enthusiastic. In fact, he sounds the most positive and upbeat that I have heard him sound for several years. He asks how the tour is going and I tell him it's fantastic. They are a great crowd and we are having tremendous fun.

'You know, Mary, you seem to enjoy it so much that perhaps you should *live* in France,' he says. It's the first time David has ever suggested such a thing.

'Well, I do love it here but I would miss the little ones too much,' I respond.

'You could always come home to visit,' he continues. 'You really should think about it.'

I find it a curious thing for him to say, given everything that has happened these last couple of years. But I am happy and relieved that he is sounding so cheerful and not his usual despondent self. I am so comforted that I even tell Jock and Jan that David is feeling great. That he is so enthusiastic about this film he really sounds just like his old self again.

But deep down I am feeling a little puzzled. It's as though something has changed. There's been a shift. A radical shift, almost overnight.

I don't get a call from David for several days. This is unusual for him, but I'm very busy with the group so I don't give it too much thought.

The tour group is to travel from the Lot to Paris for the last three days. We are to spend a whole day on the train from Gourdon to Gare d'Austerlitz and the following day go by bus to visit Monet's garden at Giverny. The rest of the time will be spent wandering around soaking up the sights and sounds of Paris. This time I am leaving from Paris to fly directly home, so I have to pack up the house and close it down for the winter before leaving. It's a bit of a logistical nightmare and I ask Jan to help out by taking the group for their last day of touring and picnicking in the countryside while I get organised to leave. Heaven knows when I will be back. The fridge has to be cleaned out, the electricity and water turned off, the shutters closed, and I also have to sort out my personal luggage – what I will leave behind and what I will carry home. It's a full day's work.

On my last day at the house, I wake early and lie on the bed for a few moments. I am filled with that certain sadness that always comes when I have to pack up and go home. But at the same time I am excited about getting back to Australia. Seeing the family, doing the book tour and hopefully sorting out my fractured life with David once and for all. While I'm still in that dozy half-awake state the phone rings and it's David. He doesn't sound like himself at all.

'What's wrong?' I ask. 'What's happened'

He speaks slowly but plainly. He says he's calling me now because he can't face saying what he needs to say in person. He says he is frightened his resolve may weaken if he tries to say what he wants to say face to face.

'It's over,' he says. 'I can't go on any more. Our marriage is finished. It's ended. I have talked it over at length with the children. They all agree it's the only solution. I'm sorry to do this to you over the phone, but I thought you should know before you left France.'

I am stunned. I can't think of a word to say.

I should have seen it coming. It's the logical conclusion to what has happened between us over the past two years. But I never really expected it would come to this. I am engulfed by a wave of sadness and I feel too numb to even cry.

I get up and start going through the motions of what needs to be done today. David is worried at my response – or lack of response – and promises to call back later. But I don't know what I will say to him. Friends are phoning to say goodbye and I tell several of them what has happened. I guess they were half expecting something like this, and they seem less shocked by the news than I am.

One friend asks a curious question: 'Do you think there could be another woman in David's life?'

My response is swift and in the negative. 'I would know if he'd met someone else. Anyway, he's been at the farm most of the time working on a script with five other people. It's just not the sort of thing David does.'

'Well,' my friend goes on to say, 'statistically, men don't leave their wives unless they have another relationship to go to. Some do, but not very often. Women, on the other hand, leave their husbands all the time, not just because they are about to embark on a new relationship. They leave for all sorts of reasons.'

I think about what's been said but don't give it much credence.

As promised, David calls during the afternoon and we talk haltingly. We both feel terribly sad and we both cry. He tells me he's sorry it has ended this way. I tell him I understand. I accept full responsibility. He insists that it's just as much his fault as it is mine. He's let me down. I tell him that I believe his decision is brave. I admit that over the last two years I have often thought I should end our marriage but simply haven't had the courage to do so. I've been too afraid of his reaction and the repercussions within the family. I thank him for being strong enough to seize the day.

We talk about the children. He tells me they also feel very sad but believe it's for the best. They are fed up with the whole situation.

Just as he is about to hang up, I ask him one final question.

'Is there someone else?'

He pauses, then says, 'No. No, there isn't anyone else. I hope someday there will be another person in my life. I certainly don't want to live alone. But at the moment there is no one else.'

I believe him.

34

 My last day at the house passes in a blur. I somehow pack my bags and clean out the house, giving away the last of my food and doing my best to put the house in order. Jan has offered to strip my bed and wash the sheets after I leave, because the train to Paris is departing early and I won't have a chance to do this one final chore.

That evening there is a slap-up dinner for the group to bid farewell to Jan and Philippe, the bus driver Claude and the beautiful Lot Valley. I shower, dress and apply my make-up. I feel somehow disembodied. It hits home that I will never be the same woman again. From this moment onwards my life is to undergo a radical change. I have defined myself for more than thirty years as a woman in a lifelong partnership with a man. Now I will be a single woman. I will live alone. I may end up living alone for the rest of my life. I have pushed my relationship with David to the brink and now it has fallen over the edge. There can be no turning back.

I join the happy group for dinner and it lifts my spirits. Jan and Philippe know what has transpired during the day and keep glancing at me with some concern. But I am doing what I have done all my life. My wide smile is there for all to see. Nobody would guess that my life has just fallen into a heap.

The train trip to Paris with the group is always fun. We take a picnic lunch that includes bottles of wine and buttery ham baguettes made by Christiane from my village, sitting back in comfort to admire the changing scenery as we speed north. The French rail system is clean, fast and efficient. Most members of the group are tired from all the walking, eating, drinking and sightseeing. At one point I look down the carriage and every one of them is sound asleep.

By mid-afternoon we are in Paris and settling into our hotel. Several in the group have never been to Paris before and it's fun to introduce them to the delights and perils of the Metro. There's nothing more thrilling than catching the Metro to the Champs Elysées and emerging from the depths of the underground railway system onto that glorious tree-lined boulevard with the Arc de Triomphe standing majestically at one end. There are gasps of joy and we set off to explore in small groups, meeting later for a meal.

I manage to escape for a couple of hours on my own. September in Paris is a beautiful month and I walk down my favourite streets and boulevards alone. I don't just walk, I stride. The sun feels warm on my skin and I catch a glimpse of myself in a shop window as I pass.

I am free. I am a free woman at last. Independent financially and emotionally. Able to make all my own decisions. I think about all the options open to me. I might just come and live in Paris for a year. It's my favourite city in the world and I would love to be here through all the seasons. Do an intensive French course. Write another book. Take a new lover. I can do whatever I want.

I am overpowered by a sense of elation. I feel exhilarated by this new perception of myself. For the past few years I have been changing. Undergoing a metamorphosis. And now, like a moth emerging from a chrysalis, I am about to fly. My wings may be a little wet, but I am on my way.

35

My sister Margaret and her husband Ken are in France on a painting holiday. One of the remarkable things I discovered when I met up with Margaret after a separation of nearly fifty years was that we had so many passions in common. France was just one of them. They are staying down on the coast, near Bordeaux, and I have organised to catch a train down and spend the day with them – not as much time as I would have liked, but better than not seeing them at all. Originally the plan was for them to come and stay for a while at Frayssinet, but their trip coincided with my tour group so they opted for a coastal village instead. They have friends sharing their rental house and they are staying in France for three weeks.

While organising the train trip to visit Margaret in Bordeaux, I realise that somehow I don't have my return plane ticket to Australia in my folder of documents. It's just three days before I am due to leave. In the confusion of that last terrible day packing up the house I must have left it behind. Normally I am quite organised about such things but I concede I must have been more shaken by David's early morning phone call than I was prepared to admit even to myself. I now have to organise an alternative ticket and get myself to Bordeaux to see Margaret – plus maintain my involvement with the tour group, who want to explore the delights of Paris again after our visit to Monet's glorious garden.

Getting a replacement international plane ticket at short notice isn't easy. Emails fly back and forth from Australia to the Paris offices of the airline company and it looks as though I will only manage to get the plane by the skin of my teeth – a new ticket can only be issued on the morning of departure. I jump on the train to Bordeaux to see Margaret wondering if I will be going home at all or if I will be stranded in Paris. I have to be at the Brisbane Writers' Festival almost immediately after I return, and there's also the issue of cost. If I miss the plane because I have lost my ticket, it's my own fault and I will have to pay for a replacement.

Being on the train soothes my nerves. I do love train travel in France. As we hurtle through the countryside, it's like an impressionist painting, all a bit blurred around the edges. Hard to spot the detail at such speed but the overall effect is beautiful. However the sensation of elation I felt the previous day has vanished. Although I am excited about seeing Margaret and Ken again, I am not looking forward to telling them that my marriage has gone wrong, and hope they won't ask too many questions. I am aware that instead of feeling strong and independent and free, as I did when striding around Paris yesterday, I am feeling rather lost and vulnerable. I tell myself this is normal in such a situation – the radical swings of emotion. It will obviously take a long time before I settle back into a pattern of feeling normal again.

Margaret and Ken are on the platform to meet me and I experience the same delight I felt last year when I saw her for the first time. But she appears to have lost weight and feels like a frail bird when I hug her. There is still a certain tentativeness about our relationship, as though we are gingerly feeling our way around each other. I imagine this is normal in such situations. Although we have shared genes and experiences with very similar childhoods in the same household, decades apart, we have not known each other as adults and there is a lot of ground to be made up. All I know is that I like her and Ken tremendously and I am thrilled to have a sister after fifty years of wondering where she was and what she was like.

We have such a happy day together, exploring a region of France I have not experienced and savouring a delicious lunch of regional specialities with their painting friends. Towards the end of our time together, I tell Margaret and Ken that I am sadly going home to a marriage breakdown. They look puzzled but ask no questions. They haven't met David and have only really just got to know me a little through my visit to them in Canada the previous year. I want to build a new relationship slowly, to fill in all the gaps of our lengthy separation, and having a marriage breakdown so soon after re-establishing contact must surely make them wonder what has been going on. It feels so strange hearing the words coming out of my mouth. It had never occurred to me that part of the whole process of separating and having a divorce is having to tell people – having to acknowledge that a lengthy relationship is about to end. I feel like a failure.

On the three-hour train journey back to Paris I am at an all-time low. Tears trickle steadily down my cheeks and I can't stem the flow. I'm sad that I only managed to see Margaret for such a few short hours and I am worried because she doesn't appear very well to me. Having just found her, I can't bear the thought that she may be ailing. I want us to be part of each other's lives for a long time to come, to make up for all those wasted years. For the first time I feel a great sense of loss for my marriage. I had been looking forward to David meeting my sister, to him also sharing in the joy of our reunion. I recall how often we lay in bed talking at night over the years, and how the subject of my lost sister often came up in our conversations. I used to say that one day I would go and find her, and he always encouraged the idea. He, of all people, understood my pain and loss. Now he may never even get to meet my sister. It's seems unbelievable. As we pull into the hectic city station at dusk, the leaden grey sky reflects my mood.

The last two days in Paris are a nightmare. In the midst of trying to wind up the tour, which has been so much fun, I am also trying to organise the replacement plane ticket. I choose an Irish pub for our farewell dinner, believing the tired travellers are a little fed up with French food. Too many feasts of duck and potatoes sautéed in goose fat. Bangers and mash and a pint or two of Guinness will make for a pleasant change. It's a fiasco. The upstairs room where we are seated is smoke-filled and after an hour we haven't even been served our first drink. I go down to the bar to try and speed things along and am rudely brushed aside by an arrogant young bartender. I lose my cool, something I seldom do, and to the amazement of my group I screech at the young man in rage. For a moment I completely lose control. The air turns blue and the male drinkers in the bar look astonished to see a well-dressed middle-aged woman in such a state of fury. I am shaken at my own behaviour and can only imagine that I must be a lot more strung out than I realised. But my tantrum does the trick, and the drinks and dinner quickly appear. I can barely swallow my food and leave most of the meal. As a parting gesture I fashion the remnants into a sculptured phallus on the plate and ask the waiter, who has been most apologetic for the appalling service, to ceremoniously present it to the barman as a parting gesture. It brings the house down.

The necessary paperwork hasn't arrived the day before I leave and the airline won't issue a new ticket. As a last resort I wait anxiously on their doorstep at nine the following morning and somehow they manage to cobble together a substitute ticket. I have to catch a taxi, which is a hellishly expensive way to get around Paris in the peak hour, and somehow I make it through check-in and customs and security – with only minutes to spare. I stagger to my seat feeling totally drained. My usual sensation of excitement at the prospect of going home has vanished. Instead I am overwhelmed by a feeling of dread.

On the plane I try to regain my perspective. I think about my life as a mother and grandmother and the way events have unfolded in my life. I had my first grandchild at the age of forty-three. I was the first of my contemporaries to become a grandparent and at the time it was considered quite unusual. I was a curiosity.

My generation – the baby boomers – had their children much later than their mothers who, in turn, had children later than their mothers before them. It's been a continuing trend, with the age of first-time motherhood gradually becoming later with each successive generation. Not that long ago a woman of twenty-eight was considered 'elderly' to start a family but now it's not unusual for women of that age to delay motherhood for another ten years. Or even longer.

I was twenty-two when my daughter Miriam was born, and she was not quite twenty-one when she gave birth to Eamonn in her last year of university. So becoming a young mother was more atypical for Miriam than it had been for me all those years ago.

I am now fifty-four and I have eight gorgeous grandchildren. Six boys and two girls. When I mention with pride my grandmotherly status, it is invariably greeted with astonishment. Not because I look particularly young for my age, but because now it is so unusual to have grandchildren at all before the age of about sixty. Let alone eight of them. What once would have been accepted as quite commonplace has become a rarity. I am in the minority and people comment on the fact that my children have all become parents at such an early age. I often think about it too.

My three biological children – daughter Miriam and sons Aaron and Ethan – all became first-time parents at twenty-one. The three pregnancies were unplanned and when discovered they were greeted with shock and disbelief followed rapidly by delight. We are not Catholic, we are not anti-abortion and the children were, I always thought, well informed about contraception. But they obviously weren't rigidly careful or concerned enough to make sure that their preventive measures were one hundred per cent. There's also the factor that instead of being considered a blight, the prospect of a baby in our family is always considered a bonus.

During their formative years I must surely have established a mindset in my children that babies equal bliss. Babies were never too much trouble or too much hard work or too expensive. They were adorable and fun and brought so much love and happiness that having one around the house was perceived as the epitome of joy. Not surprisingly, when each in turn was confronted with the prospect of parenthood they embraced rather than rejected the idea. I was quite surprised myself that they all launched into having children at such an early age. I didn't hesitate at David's suggestion that we have our first child when I was in my early twenties, but looking back I now realise I was yearning for stability and love. I knew nothing about birth or babies and I was therefore quite lucky that I took to it with such ease and pleasure.

The two boys wanting to have children at such an early age was, even under the circumstances, quite a surprise. A lot is written these days about 'Peter Pan Syndrome', where males delay commitment to relationships and parenthood until much later in their lives. Studies have shown that they would rather play with their computer games and remain living comfortably at home, rent-free, with their aging parents, than accept responsibility for starting a family. This has been blamed on the lack of positive messages in society about marriage and parenting. It is just not seen as an attractive option. But not so for our boys. They leapt into steady relationships, marriage, parenthood and mortgages all before the age when most sons even think about leaving the nest.

Our children must have been inculcated with happy messages about parenting. Those were the best years of my life, when the children were growing up, and they picked up on all those confident and positive signals. They didn't sit down and make a plan – they simply emulated the established pattern. None of them was financially secure but that didn't stop them. So, even though I was concerned about how they would cope at such tender ages with the emotional and financial implications, I was happy for them. Because they were happy. They all had good relationships with their partners and, fortunately, David and I were delighted with the choices they had made.

The whole issue of motherhood and grandmotherhood fascinates me because it has changed so dramatically in just two or three generations. I talk to other women in my age group and their experiences are so different from mine and from those of their own grandmothers. A journalist colleague in her early sixties tells me she has given up on the idea of ever becoming a grandmother. Her two children, one male and one female, both in their late thirties, show no inclination to produce offspring. When she asks them if she is ever likely to become a grand-mother, she is laughed off with the words, 'It's your problem, Mum. We're quite happy the way we are.'

So she is resigned to the probability that she may never, ever hold a grandchild.

Another friend in her late fifties with several grandchildren admits that she loves them dearly but is adamant that she has no interest in being overly involved in their lives. Certainly no interest in babysitting. 'I did the baby and kid thing for decades,' she says. 'I am free from children now and I don't want to be tied down looking after them. I love seeing them, but ultimately they are their parents' responsibility. Not mine.'

They seem harsh words but my friend is anything but cold and heartless. She adores her family. It's just that she is relishing the time she now has to do all the things she couldn't afford to do when her own children were young.

Yet another friend has a different story. Her son and daughter-in-law work full-time and she has been co-opted, with the other grandmother, into caring for the two small children several days a week. She loves them and is thrilled to be able to help, but she is also exhausted by the physical demands of looking after toddlers all day in her early sixties. She doesn't complain, however, and is just delighted that she has such a close bond with her grand-children. A bond she wouldn't have if she wasn't their carer.

I fall somewhere between the last two. I love being intimately involved in the lives of my grandchildren but I also have to be realistic because, at my age, I still work constantly and therefore don't have unlimited time to spend with them. My career involves a lot of travelling, which means I sometimes go for months without seeing them. I miss them keenly but I know that when I am back home I can balance this out in many ways. I love having them to stay at the farm, en masse, and cooking up sumptuous feasts, so that for our family sitting around the table has become the centrepiece of bringing the generations together. In the summer I take them to the swimming pool or on picnics, getting them to help prepare the food and pack the baskets.

I also love treating them to special outings – films and theatre and concerts, and trips to the big city to visit museums or the aquarium. I am aware that family outings can be very expensive and often beyond the means of their young parents, who are now all at the stage of struggling with mortgages and car payments, not to mention huge grocery bills. On a recent two-day trip to Sydney with four boys in tow – Eamonn, Sam, Theo and Hamish – I was startled at the cost of lunch in a restaurant and tickets to a live stage show. Sam, ever the observant and thoughtful one, asked me as I stuffed credit card dockets into my wallet, 'Are you thure you can afford thith Mutti?'

'Yes, Sam,' I said. 'Don't worry.'

'How much money *have* you got, Mutti?'

'Unlimited amounts,' I replied, to put his mind at ease.

I try to get to their pre-school and school open days, especially 'grandparents day', when we are given a chance to visit their classrooms, meet their teachers and see examples of their work. I went to Hamish's lovely little school in Mudgee with his other grandmother, who is about my age and also works full-time. We had both taken a day off work to attend. There was a formal assembly where the children, in class groups, performed songs and poetry. Then there were speeches. The youthful deputy principal welcomed us and emphasised how important we were in the life of these young children. He said that having grandparents who were interested and involved enough in the lives of their grandchildren to come along and support them was just fantastic. He concluded by saying: 'So I would like to thank you all for taking time out from your art classes and games of golf to come along and support your grandchildren.'

Both our hackles rose immediately. Shortly afterwards at the morning tea I took the young teacher aside and explained, quite sweetly, that not all grandmothers had time to attend art classes. Some of us had jobs and other responsibilities. Somewhat flustered, he apologised for being both ageist and sexist, and I laughed quietly to myself at his embarrassed reaction. After all, he was just conforming to the common perception. Grand-parents these days are meant to be a lot older.

Despite the fact that in generations past grandmothers were a lot younger than they are today, even back then they always seemed to be little old ladies with permed hair wearing floral frocks with lacy collars. I have seen photographs of my friend's grandmothers at fifty and sixty, and they look positively ancient in the black and white photographs of the day. I'm not that sort of grandmother – although in some ways I look forward to the day when I can feel comfortable in that more conventional, less confusing role.

In the meantime I will just enjoy my large brood and continue to set aside very special time to spend with them. After staying with Miriam and her family after their move to Adelaide, I returned home exhausted by the demands of those four lively little boys. Unpacking my bag, I found a little love letter, hidden among my clothes, from Sam. It was on pink paper cut out in the shape of a heart with the words: 'Dere Mutti, It's good to have you come down to see us. Love from Sam.'

It can't get much better than that.

$$37$$

 David is waiting patiently for me, as ever, at the exit from customs at Sydney airport. He looks tired and is a little withdrawn, kissing me affectionately but without a skerrick of passion. The total reverse of the farewell kiss he had insisted upon in front of the film crew when I was leaving for France five months ago.

In the car, before we have even exited the car park, David initiates a one-way conversation with me about the financial difficulties that lie ahead. He barely touches on the emotional issues except to say that he has made up his mind, once and for all, and that he believes this is the right and the only decision. He tells me that the long trip back to Australia, when he was forced to spend three nights alone in a hotel room in Hong Kong, was a turning point. How for that period of time he did nothing but sleep, eat and think about our damaged relationship. He says that since then he has been feeling stronger and better about himself than he has for the past three years.

I am jetlagged of course, and also emotionally exhausted. I sit and listen to David's view on how our finances will need to be managed. He doesn't believe I am capable of looking after myself financially and says he envisages maintaining his role as the 'manager' of my income and expenditure. He wants us to continue living together at the farm because we can't afford an alternative. He suggests I should seriously consider accepting any work that is offered and mentions in particular the possibility of a radio show that has been on the back burner for quite some time.

I respond by acknowledging that I have always been dis-organised in managing money and agree that, from his perspective, I am a spendthrift. However, I am not thrilled at the prospect of accepting work that will see me anchored in one place all year round. How will I be able to take the tour groups to France if I have a weekly radio job? How will I afford to live in Sydney if that is where the work is based? By the time we reach the farm we are in the throes of a heated argument and I am beginning to realise that this situation is destined to be a nightmare. I have known enough people going through messy divorces to know that the money aspect is the most problematic. And here we are at the very beginning of our dialogue and already it's shaping up unpleasantly.

The entire family is at the farm, including all our wild and woolly grandchildren. The open fires are crackling away and the air is filled with the rich aroma of Sunday lunch cooking. I am hit by a blast of warmth as I enter the kitchen and the first person I see is my daughter-in-law Lynne, mother of Isabella and now quite heavily pregnant with their second child. We make immediate eye contact and we both begin to cry. But unlike our previous reunions where we cried with happiness to see each other, our mutual tears are laden with sadness.

All I can say to her is, 'I think this is a big mistake.' She nods in agreement.

This family of mine is the most important thing in my life. Not any one individual above the others, just the group as a whole. The unit. Like many people with damaged childhoods, I had a dream to have a perfect family. And somehow I have managed to create one. There's my stepson Tony, now in his early thirties, with a successful career and a beautiful wife, Simone. A handsome and affectionate couple who are yearning to start a family because of the joy and fun they have with their nieces and nephews. Our daughter Miriam and her husband Rick, bravely wrangling their four bright and boisterous sons. A strong and committed couple with a positive outlook on life. Our blond son Aaron, less voluble than the rest, with his calm and patient wife Lorna and their two blond offspring. So different from their cousins and yet, in funny ways, so alike. Our youngest son Ethan and his partner Lynne, coping brilliantly with a disabled daughter and courageously awaiting the birth of their second child. Such an amazing group of people. Such a fantastic family. David and I as the parents and grandparents sit at the head of the table. When we sit down to lunch we number seventeen and I don't know quite how it happened.

So in spite of everything it's a happy day, simply because we are all together again. The family unit. The lunch is delicious and we drink lots of wine. The proposed separation and divorce are talked about briefly, but not in a heavy way. The children say they are sad but that it's probably going to be for the best. I try not to cry again.

Later in the day, when the family has departed, we sit alone in front of the fire for a while, listening to music and drinking wine.

'You know, David, I think this whole idea is wrong,' I say. 'I don't want to end our marriage. I never really have. I know I am to blame and I am so, so sorry that I caused you so much pain, but isn't there some way we can work this out? Surely we can resolve things between us somehow.'

His response is swift and definite. There is no possibility of reconciliation. He has made up his mind. It's over. He feels sad, but that's it. He will never, ever weaken his resolve.

Late in the evening the question of where we will sleep crops up. When he spoke to me in France, David suggested that there was no reason why we couldn't continue sleeping in the same bed. Nothing sexual, just for mutual comfort, because we were both so upset at the end of our marriage that maintaining some closeness might help. At the time I found the notion strange and said it would be much more cut and dried if from the outset we slept in separate rooms. Now I am feeling the reverse; that I would like to be close to him. In my heart I am thinking that if we physically touch it may help to bridge the gap. Perhaps if we make love, his resolve may even soften. But he has made up the spare room for himself. We will be sleeping apart.

When I wake in the morning, I am momentarily convinced that the whole thing was just a dream. I have imagined it. I can't possibly be getting divorced from David. He brings me tea and bread with butter in bed as he has done for so many years and I find myself incapable of speaking. A numbness has descended.

David has to drive to Sydney for a funeral. It gives me a day to wander around the house and the farm recovering from my jetlag. David is a great one for taking down phone messages on scraps of paper and leaving them lying around for weeks, sometimes months, at a time. By the phone in the kitchen I find an old envelope with a list of messages. Some are obviously messages from me because I recognise the times I have called from France. He writes 'my love' as the name of the person calling. Then at the end of the list are two messages written at times that could not possibly have been from me. I would have been in transit. For the caller he has written 'my other love'. I ponder for a moment then phone him on his mobile.

'Who is this "other love" person?' I ask.

He is uncomfortable and can't speak. He's in a noisy pub with a large crowd of friends. It's the wake. He laughs it off, but I still feel unsettled by it. *Other love.* What does it mean? But when he gets back late that night, I am already asleep.

I have an appointment the following day with a specialist in Orange because my throat has been giving me problems. My voice sometimes sounds harsh and gravelly and I am concerned I may have grown nodules on my vocal cords – a common problem for singers and people like me who talk a lot. As I am scheduled to give more than ten speeches – including several lengthy literary lunches – during the book promotional tour, I am worried that my voice won't last the distance. It's more than an hour's drive to Orange and David insists on taking me.

'No matter what happens between us, I want to be around to support you,' he says.

In the car I am again incapable of saying much. I really don't know what to say any more. As we drive along he starts another conversation, somewhat hesitantly.

'You know how you were asking me about that message beside the phone yesterday?' he starts. 'The "other love" message? And do you remember when we were talking on the phone in France and you asked if there was someone else?'

'Mmm,' I say.

'Well, there is someone else. It's not definite yet. Nothing's actually happened. But I'm happy because I have the possibility of a new relationship.'

Total silence from me.

The words tumble out. When I was in France, he was phoned by a South African woman writer who was put in contact with him by some of the filmmakers he worked with during the 1980s. She was visiting eastern Australia for a few days and David offered to show her around. She visited the farm briefly and he drove her around the local countryside. He also showed her the sights of Sydney.

On the day she was returning to Africa he drove her to the airport. Out of the blue she made a declaration of love to him. He couldn't have been more surprised. She told him that from the moment she first saw him she felt overwhelmed and that she was convinced she was in love with him. Totally. Love at first sight. During her visit he had screened the 'Australian Story' documentary and she had been deeply affected by it. Moved and filled with compassion for his situation. They spent a few moments in the car holding each other and kissing before she left.

He was overwhelmed. At the moment in his life when he felt at his lowest ebb, when his wife of thirty-three years had betrayed him not once but twice, when he felt his self-esteem had hit rock bottom, somebody had fallen madly in love with him. It had turned his life, and mine, upside down.

38

Sitting in the doctor's waiting room, I am light-headed and disorientated. I have sent David away to wait for me in the car. I can't stand the thought of being near him, but I don't quite know why. It's a strange sensation when you are hit with a piece of information that is so powerful and so painful to assimilate that you feel disembodied. I suppose it was just how David felt when he first discovered I was having an affair in France. Stunned with disbelief. Finally I understand. For two years, David has been asking me to put myself in his shoes; to imagine how he must be feeling, and I couldn't. Now I can.

The doctor is efficient and speaks with a strong South African accent. I have to swallow a tiny camera inserted through my right nostril so he can examine my throat in detail. He tells me my throat and vocal cords are perfectly healthy, it's just that I must have been dehydrated which has caused the vocal cords to dry out. I need to drink lots of water during the day to wash them clean and prevent them from drying out again. The long hot summer in France probably contributed to my symptoms.

I ask him where he is from and he tells me Johannesburg. I immediately start telling him about *Mapantsula*, the anti-apartheid film David made there in 1987. As I speak, tears start rolling down my cheeks. Here I am telling this doctor – a total stranger – about my husband, of whom I am so proud. Telling him about a film that was selected for the Cannes Film Festival and won for David an Australian Human Rights Film Award.

But he's no longer my husband. He's my ex-husband. And soon he will probably be somebody else's husband. I have lost him and I have nobody to blame but myself.

Why am I so shocked by what has just happened? Surely this is what I should have expected. Should have known would happen. It is the logical outcome of the situation I created. It is what I deserve, given my outrageous behaviour and reckless disregard for David and for our marriage. I am getting my comeuppance. My just desserts. How could I have imagined that David would just sit quietly on the sidelines and wait for me to get my wild sexual urges out of my system? How could I have ignored the fact that he had been devastated and humiliated about every aspect of the last three years? The affairs. The book. The documentary. I have been selfish and self-centred and arrogant. So arrogant that I took for granted that David would not ever be interested in another woman. That any other woman would fall in love with him.

I have been a fool. And now I am to pay the price.

<h1 style="text-align:center">39</h1>

 In the car on the way back from Orange we have the most terrible fight we have ever had in our lives together. We've had some pretty passionate rows over the years, but nothing to touch this. To this day I can't remember exactly what is said or what sparked his outburst, but it is terrifying in its intensity. I have no idea how David doesn't crash the car or have a heart attack. For the first time ever he expresses his anger about what has happened. A part of him now hates me so vehemently that I am convinced he could kill me, he feels it so deeply. His words are like a thousand knives cutting into my flesh and they go on and on for miles and miles as he drives. Slicing through me.

He wants me to leave. Now. Pack my bags immediately and get out. Go. He wants never to see me again. So many things have driven him to this point of fury. Not just the two affairs but the fact that I didn't tell him about being attacked by the Englishman. That I have had unprotected sex with my two lovers and therefore put not just myself but also him at risk of catching a sexually transmitted disease. That I have seemed oblivious to his pain. That I have ignored his heartfelt letters. He goes on and on and calls me names so terrible that I could never ever repeat them.

When the car pulls into the farm shed I turn and grab hold of him. We are both shaking and crying. I just hold him and hold him and say I can't go now. I will go, but not now. I can't leave him in this terrible state. I am frightened for him. I am frightened for both of us. I cling to him and slowly he starts to calm down. To breathe more normally. We have passed through the eye of the storm and are now on the other side.

It's getting late. I prepare a simple meal with the little energy I can muster and we shadow each other, barely speaking. Going through the motions. Trying to regain a little normality. After dinner and a few glasses of wine, we start to unwind a little more. I light the fire in the sitting room and we sit together. He tells me that he has phoned his woman friend in South Africa to tell her that he has told me the full story. They had apparently agreed that they would keep their developing relationship to themselves until after we had formally separated or divorced. They wanted it considered as a separate issue to our marriage breakdown. From David's perspective they are two entirely different events and not connected in any way.

After the shattering events of this afternoon, I am consumed by a desire for closeness to David. As if some tenderness between us will somehow help expunge the horror of our fight. I move close to him on the sofa and put my arms around him. We kiss and speak softly, both apologising for the terrible scene, for the hatred and the anger and the bitter words. I desperately want to make love. Not to reclaim David from the arms of his new lover but for my own comfort. A balm to smooth away some of the pain. David draws back and says it's now impossible for him to make love to me. That he can never make love to me again. He has promised his new woman that there will be no intimacy between us. He is saving his love for her.

David was my first true lover. Although I had a serious teenage boyfriend whom I loved deeply for three years before I met David, it was an immature relationship. Certainly it was less than satisfactory sexually, although I didn't realise it at the time. When you haven't had an orgasm you don't know what one feels like. You don't realise what you are missing out on.

David was eleven years older than me and had been through a ten-year marriage and many lovers. His maturity and experience were a revelation to me and I was totally engulfed by the joy of sex for the first time. The first few years we were together we made love every single day, sometimes more than once. It was an intense intimacy the like of which I had never experienced. In every sense David introduced me to the ways of love. His tenderness released me from inhibition and his passion freed me from the fears I had about my own sexual inadequacies. I had low self-esteem and a negative body image. David made me feel beautiful and desirable for the very first time.

Throughout our lives together our sexual bond remained strong. Through lengthy separations when David was away working. Through pregnancies, births and breast-feeding. Through the trials and tribulations of raising four children from toddlerhood to adulthood while managing two demanding careers. We certainly didn't make love every day as we had once when young and first in love, but the passion still remained. I took it for granted. I suppose he took it for granted too.

Now David is planning to take his passion to another woman. He doesn't want me any more. Not sexually and not emotionally. I have destroyed his feeling for me and thereby have lost the most significant person in my life.

40

I wake with a start at two in the morning and the events of the preceding day come flooding back to me. I lie rigidly in the bed sorting through the sequence of events. The drive to Orange. David's confession about his new relationship. My emotions in the doctor's surgery. The terrible fight in the car. The dinner. My attempted seduction, his rejection of me and his promise of fidelity to the new woman.

Somehow during my short sleep a very different emotion has taken hold. Gone is the sadness, the pain, the guilt, the remorse, the regret. I am seized by an anger so intense that I can barely lie still. I am furious. I am incensed. I am outraged. How could David do this to me? How could he leave me for another woman? How could he stop loving me, just like that, and go off into the sunset with somebody else? How could he?

Now this is where I find it difficult to justify my response to the situation in which I find myself. Common sense dictates that David is just behaving the way any normal person would under the circumstances. His wife has been unfaithful to him not with one man but with two. His wife has disregarded his pain for three years and has behaved in a wilful and selfish manner. His wife has done nothing but point out his flaws and his short-comings and has attempted to blame him for her philandering. His wife has written a book in which she has described him as an absent father and a husband who didn't satisfy her emotional needs. His wife has dumped on him big time. And now he has the opportunity for a new life with a new love and he's going for it. Who could blame him and what right has she to be angry about it?

But angry I am. Wild with rage. I lie awake for the rest of the night, seething. We have to catch an early flight to Sydney from Bathurst, because my book tour is about to begin. The first event on the itinerary is the Brisbane Writers' Festival; David has meetings with various film partners in Queensland and has booked a flight to travel with me. He will stay for the duration of the festival then come back to Sydney with me for the major event of the tour, a literary lunch at the Sheraton Hotel. I will then travel accompanied by the Pan Macmillan publicist, Jane Novak, to Perth. All up the tour will last for more than three weeks and the schedule she has emailed me is gruelling.

I wonder how I am going to cope with it all. I have to make speeches, dozens of them, to large groups and I have to look glamorous and appear confident and upbeat. On top of my life. But David is leaving me, my life is in tatters and I am completely demented. The timing couldn't be worse.

I get up before dawn and finishing packing my suitcase. In anticipation of the tour I have been shopping in France and have brought out some new clothes and shoes. It's strange for me to spend a lot of money on clothes. Shoes in particular. My entire adult life I have bought one new pair of shoes a year and worn them until they have fallen apart. In one shopping spree in Cahors I bought seven pairs of shoes, from sexy sandals to stilettos. I can barely fit them all in the suitcase.

Before David has even emerged from the spare room, I have dressed, applied my make-up and put my bags in my car. In my rage I have also hidden his partial denture. David played rugby and boxed in his youth and his front teeth have broken off. Without the denture he has great gaps in his mouth and in my irrational state I hide the teeth so that he will have to travel to Brisbane and attend all his meetings without them. At the time it seems like a great idea.

As he comes out to make the coffee and tea I head for the back door.

'What are you doing?' he asks, rubbing his eyes. 'Where are you going?'

'I am going to Bathurst to wait for the plane. See you at the airport.'

'But we're not due there for two hours or more. Are you mad or something?'

I let him have it with both barrels. Mad isn't the word. Without raising my voice, but through tightly clenched teeth, I explain why I am so angry.

'For the past three years we have both been through hell. I have struggled with myself because, even though I fell in love with another man, I was determined to hang on to our marriage. I couldn't leave you. I wouldn't leave you no matter what. Even during the second affair I always intended to stay married to you. I was hoping you would never find out, but you did. And I don't blame you for being hurt and angry and bitter.

'What I am trying to say is that in spite of everything that happened, I always wanted to hang on to our marriage. I could never, ever have just left you.'

At this moment he speaks over me. Sharply. 'Well you could have fooled me. I thought the reason for the affairs was that you wanted to end the marriage. That you had the affairs in order to end the marriage. That you just didn't have the guts to come out and say it.'

'Not true,' I counter. 'And after all we've been through you are now going to walk out and leave me for someone you barely know. Someone you spent time with over a period of five days. *Five days!* You don't *know* this woman. You don't really know anything about her. But you are prepared to throw away our thirty-three-year relationship for someone who kissed you in a car and said she loved you. I'm not the one who is mad. It's you.'

I dash out the door and head for Bathurst, leaving David standing like a stunned mullet in the kitchen dressed in his checked nightshirt. When we went to bed last night, we had been warm and affectionate with each other. We had a late-night hug and apologised yet again for our ghastly fight. Now this morning he has been confronted by a raging virago. A woman obviously not in control of her senses. And it's me.

$\mathcal{41}$

 I arrive on Miriam and Rick's doorstep in Bathurst at 7.15 a.m. I have never dropped in unannounced at this time of day before but they welcome me in and make a fresh pot of tea. I am pacing the floor and telling Miriam how angry I am with her father, and why I am so angry. She doesn't proffer an opinion one way or the other but laughs in amazement when I tell her I have hidden his teeth. She gives me an odd look, as though she thinks I've lost my marbles.

The phone rings and it's David. Rick looks at me but I indicate that I don't want to talk, so he acts dumb. David tells him that I have gone mad and that he can't find his teeth. He tells Rick he believes I have done something with them.

'If she turns up,' he says, 'get her to call me straight away.'

The little boys are starting to come out of their bedrooms and look a bit surprised to see me all dressed up and made-up in their kitchen so early in the morning. I think perhaps I should leave them in peace. It isn't fair to involve them in our messy problem. So I give them all hugs and kisses and promise to call from every city I visit to keep them up to date with what I am doing.

There's enough time to drive back to the farm. It's better if we travel to the airport in one car, so I allow common sense to override my temporary insanity. I drive home, tell David where his teeth have been stashed and we drive back together to the airport. He tries talking with me, reasoning with me, but I am still too angry to speak. I have never experienced high blood pressure but I think I must be having it now. My eyes feel like they are about to pop out of my head. My muscles feel taut and tense and my skin is pressing in on me, holding me together. Barely.

The two flights from Bathurst to Brisbane are a blur. We must have checked in and been issued boarding passes and passed through security but I have no recollection of any of it. We don't sit together on the planes and we nearly miss each other at the other end, even though we are meant to be travelling together. David has quickly phoned a friend on his mobile to see if he can stay with him for the three nights of our visit rather than at the hotel where we have been booked by the organisers of the festival. I have made it perfectly clear that I don't want him anywhere near me. At the baggage carousel I see him waiting for his bag. He is talking on his mobile again, confirming his meeting. I walk over to speak to him and as I approach I suddenly go blank. My knees buckle and I fall in a heap on the floor. My blackout must have only been momentary but it is enough to give us both a big fright.

David hails a taxi to get me to the hotel and just as it pulls out from the kerb I tell the driver to stop and beg David to stay with me tonight because I am feeling so shaken by what has just happened. How can I get up and perform on a stage in front of a large audience when I can barely put one foot in front the other? I have never felt more vulnerable and frightened.

I lie on the bed and manage to sleep for several hours in the afternoon while David goes to his first meeting. We have been left a message at reception asking us to meet with the publicist, Jane, and some of the other authors for dinner. I somehow have to pull myself together to get through the next few weeks. If I am a total cot case on day one, I can't imagine how I am going to be by the end of the tour.

David is more tender and concerned than I could have imagined, given my behaviour of this morning. He has never seen me in such a state and it has obviously caused him grave concern. We don't talk any more about our situation and he helps me get myself together in time for the dinner. Anyone who didn't know me probably wouldn't pick up on the fact that I am in such a bad way that first night. I am just a little quieter and more thoughtful than usual. More subdued. I manage to find a moment to mumble to Jane that David and I are going through a very rocky time. I think I should warn her in case things take a turn for the worse.

In retrospect it was a wise move, alerting her to my fragility, because over the next few weeks as we tour from one side of the country to the other Jane is my rock. The only person really who keeps me going.

42

So here we are in a hotel room in Brisbane in bed together again. Clinging to each other as we fall into a sleep of nervous and physical exhaustion. In the middle of the night I wake up and find myself with my arms wrapped warmly around my husband. My old lover. The man I would certainly have shot through the forehead this morning if I had been unfortunate enough to own a gun. I run my hand down his chest, over his belly and into his groin. He stirs. I know exactly what I am doing. I am seducing him and it feels very strange that after all these years I need to convince him that he should make love to me. But he doesn't seem to need much convincing. It's what he told me he was afraid of. That if we were together again, if we fell back into intimacy, he would be incapable of resisting. Sex is a great way to relieve tension, to bring about a feeling of wellbeing. But this is much, much more than that for me. It is like a valve being opened on a pressure cooker. As though all the build-up of emotions over the last few days – not to mention weeks, and months and years – have suddenly been released. I cry with the sheer absolution of it. Surely this must mean we are okay. There is hope. We can go on. Surely we are destined to stay together.

We both sleep well afterwards but in the morning the tide has turned. David is now angry both with me and himself. Very angry. I have made him break his promise to the new woman in his life. She doesn't realise he is staying here at the hotel with me, she thinks he is staying with friends. Now not only has he lied to her about his whereabouts, he has made love to me. He is distraught.

'I know you say I don't know this woman, but I know a lot more than you think. We have talked on the phone every day since she left and we know a lot about each other. She is a lovely person and I care about her a lot. I would rather die than hurt her. I will not hurt her.'

I have to appear on a panel later in the morning with several other authors and I beg him to calm down so I can get on with what is expected of me. I fear that if our discussion escalates into another furious row, I will be incapable of continuing. He has more film meetings so we go our separate ways. Over morning tea I fill Jane in on what's been happening then go on to the panel session, which is a lot of fun and very well received. Perhaps the pressure of the tour will be good for me. Take my mind off things and give me an alternative focus. I hope so.

David and I stop talking about our troubles and just try our best to enjoy being part of the festival. There are interesting sessions to attend and a range of social events that are an ideal distraction. I meet his film colleagues and he meets up with lots of the other authors. Festivals are always fun, and we throw ourselves into this one with great enthusiasm. We also make love whenever we are alone together. Like we did when we first fell in love all those decades ago. The threat of his leaving me for another woman has made me desire him more than I have for years. And for him, I sense, it's as though it's our last opportunity to demonstrate to each other our old but somehow enduring love. As though we are offering comfort to each other in time of extreme pain and stress.

We travel back to Sydney for the big literary luncheon and, thank heavens, I am feeling steady again. More in control of myself and my emotions. In a taxi from the airport to the hotel, David's mobile phone beeps to tell him that he has a message. He listens to it and because we are in such close proximity I can hear the voice of the caller. It's the new woman. And there are several messages. One after the other. I gaze discreetly in the other direction, out of the taxi window, but I can clearly hear her voice and it fills me with pain. I am starting to hate her and that really isn't fair. None of this is her fault. It's mine. But I need to understand who she is and why she wants my husband.

I am jealous. Really jealous. And it's an emotion I have never experienced before in my life. It doesn't feel nice.

Part of my jealousy is that the woman is younger than me. Eight years younger, which makes her nearly nineteen years younger than David. I recall vividly David's anger at my taking a younger lover. How poignantly I now understand. Why age should make such a difference I don't really know. But it does.

David leaves me at the hotel and flies back to the farm for the night. In the morning, early, he and Miriam will drive back to the city for the big literary lunch and afterwards Miriam will fly back home to her family. In the hotel room I lie on the bed and my imagination races with thoughts of David and the woman. He'll probably talk to her on the phone the minute he gets back home to the farm. Glad to be away from me so he can speak to her. He must have lied about where he's been staying and I know his mobile phone has been switched off when we are together, in case she calls. It's what happens when deception creeps into relationships. The tangled web. Life is suddenly complicated. It certainly was for me with my lovers in France and now it is for him. What a mess I have created.

The irony of my situation doesn't escape me but I can see no humour in it at all. Somehow I have to convince David that he's making a big mistake and that we should try and salvage our relationship and our marriage. But how can I change his mind? He is resolute. So determined.

I have an early night and take a sleeping pill in the hope that I will crash out and be refreshed for the big day ahead of me. I have to be at Channel 9 first thing for an interview on the Kerri-Anne show, then back at the hotel by noon for the big literary lunch. More than seven hundred bookings have been taken, so it's going to be one of the most important events of the tour.

I do manage a good night's sleep and feel quite sparky by the time Jane picks me up to go to the television station. The interview goes well and we are back at the hotel with more than an hour to spare. David and Miriam arrive and we have a cup of tea in the room before going down to the ballroom for the lunch. The room is packed with well-dressed women of a certain age. My age. And there are several familiar faces, including my niece Louise, my best friend Christine and some of the women who have been on my last couple of walking tours. After the main course I am introduced by the literary editor of the *Sydney Morning Herald*, Malcolm Knox. He says all the usual things – a bit of background about my career – then welcomes me onto the stage with the words: 'It is therefore with great pleasure that I introduce to you the well-known author and adulterer Mary Moody.'

There is an audible gasp from the audience and they react to Malcolm's introduction by cheering me onto the stage. In a way, it's a fitting start to the tour. A barometer of how differently my book is being received by men and women. Even though his remark is not meant to be taken seriously – it's just a throwaway line – it has created a ripple of outrage and gives me a perfect footing to launch into my speech. I love giving talks because I get such a warm and spontaneous reaction from the audience. I never quite know what I am going to say but I have the fortunate ability to be able to sense the mood of a room and then pitch my talk accordingly.

The way I speak is very much like the way I write. Straight down the line, forthright, candid and hopefully sometimes funny. Every so often I glance down to David and make eye contact. It seems weird that he is sitting there listening to me tell all these women about my adventures in France, including the affair, and about how supportive he has been of me through the rollercoaster of the last few years. I can't imagine any other man in the world feeling comfortable sitting in a crowded room hearing his wife speak about her infidelity. But he does – in fact he claims to enjoy my talks no matter what the topic. I try not to think about the fact that some of the words I am speaking have a hollow ring to them. Nobody in the room, apart from Miriam, my friend Christine and Jane, knows the truth of our situation. That our marriage is over. It's all too difficult at this stage – at the launch of the book – to flatten the audience with such a negative message.

At the end of my talk I sign books and I am thrilled by the length of the queue and the enthusiasm of everyone who approaches the table with a book to be signed. I also notice that David has been cornered by a large group of women and he is signing their copies of the books too. How bizarre is this? The wronged husband autographing copies of his unfaithful wife's confessional book. I feel as though our lives are no longer our own. That by committing my story to paper and putting it out into a public place I have forfeited any right to or hope of privacy. The implications are appalling.

When you write a story from life candidly, as I have done, it invites people to talk openly about their feelings, which can be a good thing. It can also be a bit confronting and at times even distressing. I realise that by sharing my own experiences, both good and bad, readers are going to identify with certain issues that I raise and then if they come to hear me speak, they will ask questions, make comments or share their own experiences. Giving a talk is almost like mass group therapy, and I never quite know what to expect.

A lot of women share their pain with me. I have written openly about having an affair and about cheating on my husband. But usually the shoe is on the other foot and I am frequently approached by women whose husbands have been unfaithful to them. Often they say that they were expecting to dislike me or to hate my book but have been pleasantly surprised to find that I am not some kind of monster. Some hard-hearted witch. Because it's natural for them to project their anger onto someone who has behaved in the same way as the partner who has caused them so much pain.

At one speaking event a man approaches me clutching a copy of *Last Tango*. He starts to cry and alarm bells go off inside my head. The words spill out. His wife is having an affair. She has also been reading my book. Thank heavens he quickly tells me that the affair began before she read the book and not afterwards. I do fear that by writing about my journey I am somehow giving permission for others to go down the same path. I'm certainly not – my books are not guide books to navigating the challenges of mid-life or manuals on how to manage extra-marital relationships. They are simply my own story and presented more as a cautionary tale than a solution to life's problems. The weeping man says he has come to hear me speak and wants to know if David will be at the lunch. He wants to talk to him. Fortunately David isn't at this particular event, because I know he would feel great compassion but also a deep sense of inadequacy. We are not counsellors. We are not trained to help people who are unhappy or in crisis. It's a common problem, I expect, for people who have written books that touch raw nerve endings.

Sometimes women come up to me to tell me that their husbands left them for another woman. Sometimes they left them for a man. Most women say they have coped and a lot express the view that their lives have improved dramatically since their marriages have ended. That they have found a new life for themselves, often a new and much more satisfying relationship. I suppose that because I write and speak in a friendly manner people see me as approachable, which I certainly am. But sometimes their stories hit a raw nerve with me. Touch me deeply and make me realise that I am not the only person struggling through the difficulties of life and love.

At an evening event where I am to be the after-dinner speaker, an attractive woman in her late fifties is seated opposite me. We chat merrily through the meal and have a lot in common. Children, grandchildren, a love of travel and of reading. After I have given my talk, I sit back at the table and she tells me her story.

'My husband left me almost ten years ago, for a younger woman. Much younger,' she says.

I must have looked concerned. She reassures me. 'It's fine now,' she continues. 'I have a new man and he's just lovely. We are very, very happy. My ex-husband has a couple of young children and he finds them exhausting. I think he's lonely. He phones me often just for a chat on some sort of pretext and then wants to talk about old times and about our old friends and family.

'Recently one of our mutual friends – the best man at our wedding – died. We were both upset, obviously. But he couldn't share his feelings with his new wife. It didn't mean very much to her, that connection. He needed to call me to talk about his sadness, because he knew I would understand.

'I hated him when he left, because he left me for sex with a younger woman. But now I just feel sorry for him. I think he often feels lost.'

Her story haunts me. I understand exactly the sense of what she is trying to convey. That even though she and her ex-husband are both in new relationships, something wonderful had been lost when they separated.

The fact that David sometimes comes along to my talks is unsettling for some people. The ABC radio 'Books and Writing' presenter Ramona Koval did a breakfast chat session with me in Brisbane where we sat on stools in front of an audience and discussed the book, then I answered questions from the floor. Afterwards Ramona said she found it strange having David sitting in the front row, and felt that it had probably inhibited some of the questions that might otherwise have been asked by the audience. But my experience has been quite different. Women seem to be intrigued by David's presence when I speak openly about our experiences. They often mob him after a talk and want to discuss various issues with him. He usually finds the attention quite amusing, although sometimes also quite unsettling. He gets into quite lengthy debates with some of these women about their perceptions. They often praise him for being so tolerant and he explains that he has, indeed, been very hurt and angry at times. But it seems they would all like a supportive husband who will not only stick by his wife no matter what, but also be prepared to face up to a public audience when most men would cringe or run away.

The whole issue of this public scrutiny is summed up beautifully at the Norfolk Island Writers' Festival by one of the other authors. We are having lunch not long after one of my sessions, where David had been surrounded by a group of enthusiastic women readers after the talk.

'You're the hero of this festival,' the writer says to David with a wry smile. 'Much more admired than any of us authors. Every woman in the room wants a man like you. Who will love his wife even if she runs off to France and has an affair.'

We giggle but know it's a long way from the truth. David has not enjoyed any aspect of this public saga. At times he feels that we are like a couple of circus freaks, displaying ourselves for the scrutiny of strangers. I have a more sanguine view: that we are no different from our audience in our hopes and dreams and aspirations. That if we can, by being totally open and honest, demonstrate that we are walking the same rocky path so many others are also treading, then it can't be such a bad thing.

The reaction of journalists and interviewers to my last book has been mixed. Most reviews have been positive, although some have been quite brutal in their damnation. The reaction of women writers is quite different from men. Two female reviewers: 'She speaks for a generation of women and her writing is full of the joys of birth and death and everything in between.' 'I have never read a more honest account of the ups and downs of this sort of enterprise. Don't let me spoil it for you. My heart went out to her when she confessed to being just a tiny bit bored with gardening.'

And one male reviewer: '. . . her action-packed French social life is chronicled, but Moody's reflections on it are so shallow and her self absorption so total that it all blurs to a series of lifestyle choices (if I want to, why not?).'

Ouch! It's what I should have expected given that I was picking apart my long-term marriage in public and perhaps posing a threat to some men who feel uncomfortable with women's honesty. I have similar reactions when I do media interviews. The women journalists are usually enthusiastic about the book and identify strongly with the themes and my conclusions. The men are usually more reserved and sometimes a little aggressive. Shock jocks in particular.

One of the biggest surprises is George Negus. I am flown to Melbourne to do his now defunct early evening show to record an interview on the theme of 'escape'. About my reasons for running away to France. The midlife desire for freedom and change. All the usual questions, I assume.

But no. Halfway through the interview, George changes tack. He opens the book at a marked page and starts to read: 'My filmmaking husband David is a passionate man who can be exasperating to live with because of his entrenched attitudes towards all aspects of life. He's not a flexible or easygoing person in any sense and we have clashed almost constantly for the past thirty-one years over all sorts of trivial and day-to-day incidents and concerns. He is inclined to get upset about things that most people would regard as unimportant and he is a man with a strong sense of routine and order, baulking at spontaneity or unexpected change. He just likes things the way they are because it makes him feel secure.'

George then launches into a bit of an attack. 'What gives you the right to say these things about your husband?' he asks with furrowed brows. 'Why do you need to write about your marriage this way?'

Somewhat stunned at the change of direction in the interview, I simply ask George if he has actually read the whole book.

'Well, no,' he admits. 'I've dipped into it. But I do have a strong impression of what you are writing about.'

'Well that's not good enough George,' I respond, somewhat thin-lipped. 'If you had gone on to finish reading that same chapter, I said some absolutely wonderful things about my husband David. You can't just pluck a few sentences and use them out of context. It's a whole book about a whole story. And if you were to ask my husband, who has read the whole book several times, he would tell you he can't deny anything I have said. He mightn't necessarily like me saying it, but it's the truth.'

Abashed, George switches back to the original line of questioning. When the interview is finally edited and put to air, that small segment does not appear. It was embarrassing for both of us, but it does illustrate the sort of attitude that some men have towards women who are brave or mad enough to write and talk about the way they really feel.

After the Sydney literary lunch David and I have only one night together before I leave in the morning for Perth and the rest of the tour. I'm feeling quite desperate. Somehow I have to turn things around between now and when we go our separate ways in the morning. We go back up to the room and David decides he'll have a work-out in the hotel gym. We then plan to have a late afternoon snooze and go out for a quiet dinner together. David has been keeping his mobile phone by his side at all times, even taking it to the gym, so while he is having a shower after his work-out I call out to him that I am going down to the shops for a little while. I steal the phone from his bedside table and make a hasty exit. I don't own a mobile phone and I don't even understand how they work, except to press the red and green buttons for calls. But I know they have a memory and somewhere in this phone are calls from the new woman. I need to hear her voice. I want to know what messages she has been leaving him. I need to understand.

I sit on a bench in Pitt Street Mall and fumble with the

phone trying to work out how to access the message bank. After several botched attempts I work it out and I hold it tightly to my ear as message after message from her plays back to me. Her voice is soft and low and she speaks with an intimacy that shocks me. She calls him darling and expresses concern for his wellbeing. Is he getting enough sleep? Is he feeling upset or unhappy? Is he coping with his difficulties (meaning me, I suppose)? I play them back a second time with tears pouring from my eyes. Then I play them a third time just to be sure that I haven't missed anything.

Back at the hotel room David is waiting for me, furious. He realises what I have done and asks me to return his phone immediately. I'm hurt, I'm sad, I'm jealous, I'm frightened and I'm angry. All at the same time. David and the woman have obviously accelerated their relationship much further than I thought. It's way past the kissing in the car stage.

We talk and talk but I'm not really capable of a rational discussion. I ask a lot of questions, in particular about his future plans with her. He says he will go to South Africa in February and will live with her for a while. They will test the waters and see how they like each other. He has made a commitment to her. A total commitment. He has told her his marriage is over. Finished. That he is ready for a new relationship. With her. She has told him that she wants to spend the rest of her life with him. She is convinced he is the one for her. Her future.

I try everything I can to make him change his mind. But nothing has even the slightest impact. We make love, but that doesn't soften his resolve. We talk about our family and our love for them. He doesn't weaken. We talk about the farm and our financial and emotional ties to it. It makes no difference. I cry.

I plead. I get angry and say horrible things about the woman. I threaten to call her. I sob. He simply will not budge.

I guess we finally get some sleep. I don't really remember. I have to leave with Jane very early in the morning for an interview on breakfast television. Then we fly to Perth, where I have a literary event in the evening. It's going to be a long, arduous day and I am totally shattered.

At the television station at 7 a.m., make-up and hair in place, I sit quietly in the waiting room with Jane before being ushered into the studio for my interview. Jane senses how fragile I am. There is a monitor with the program we are doing playing live-to-air. Mel and Kochie with their usual humorous banter.

Mel throws to the commercial break with the words: 'After the break we'll be talking about having an affair and getting away with it by someone who knows.'

The words don't seem to impinge on my numb brain, but Jane is on her feet in a flash, dashing out to find the producer of the show. Words are exchanged but it is too late to change the line of questioning. At least I am forewarned that it's going to be a rocky ride. Like a lamb to the slaughter, they lead me to the sofa where the interview is about to start. I wonder how on earth I'm going to handle it.

David Koch opens the interview brightly with a brief intro-duction. Then: 'Well, Mary, you've just had an extra-marital affair. Would you recommend it?'

Blam. Right between the eyes.

'Don't be mad,' I respond, trying my best to look amused rather than amazed. 'It was the most traumatic event of my life and I am still trying to deal with the repercussions.'

I then steer the interview away from the affair by talking with great enthusiasm about other aspects of the book. The food in France. The farm at Bathurst. My grandchildren.

It works. We end on a happy note and there are no more heart-lurching questions to field. As we leave the studio, I wonder if David has been watching me on the hotel television. Probably.

Back at the hotel I finish packing and we say our goodbyes. He holds me closely and tells me that no matter what happens he will always love me. I ask him to think seriously about everything we have discussed. I tell him I am as worried about him and his future as I am about myself. And I mean it.

'There is still so much about our relationship that is good,' I say as I prepare to leave. 'Too good to just throw away. Our lives are intertwined. We mustn't unravel them. We must at least give our marriage one more try.'

He says nothing and I leave for Perth.

45

 The first few publicity events in Sydney – the interviews and the lunch – have prepared me for the sort of questions I am going to have to face on this tour. Jane has been very careful in selecting media reporters who will be positive, but we are both still worried that I will have to counter some tricky interrogation along the way. This was something that didn't really occur to me when I was writing the book, but now I see that I have stirred up a bit of a hornet's nest and I am going to have to deal with the consequences of my frankness.

The literary event in Perth is a cocktail party rather than a dinner, with several hundred well-dressed women milling around sipping champagne and eating finger food when I arrive. The bar closes and the audience is ushered into a small auditorium. A couple of women have hijacked the last of the champagne and have the bottles hidden under their seats. They keep drinking while I give the talk, laughing more uproariously than the rest of the audience. Then it comes to question time.

A few typical questions pertaining to French food and the progress of my language skills are asked. Then one of the closet champagne drinkers lurches to her feet.

'Gidday Mary,' she slurs slightly. 'Loved both your books and I also saw the documentary on the ABC. What I reckon is that you should leave your husband. He's boring. Go back to France and have another affair. Have lots of affairs. Good on you, Mary.'

How do I handle this one? I try to make light of it without totally brushing her aside with: 'Well, it's not that easy really. I love my husband and I don't want to leave him. I value him and our family too much to abandon them. And I might get bored if I was in France all the time. I will always have the desire to come home again.'

If only they knew the truth.

In between bookstore signings and literary events I give radio interviews constantly, sometimes in a studio and sometimes over the phone from the hotel room. Jane has organised a pretty hectic schedule so I don't have much time to sit around dwelling on my problems. But in the evenings I phone David and from the first day he sounds different. More distant. Less receptive. Now that I am away from him, physically at a distance, he has regained his strength and his resolve. Whenever I mention the issue of us 'trying again', he says no. He's made up his mind. He will live with me at the farm until February so that we can have our last Christmas together as a family, then he will go to meet up with the other woman.

He keeps telling me I should go and live in France full-time. He says he wants to keep the farm for the family – in particular for our son Ethan, who has been establishing a native plant nursery on the property. I will be welcome, he says, to come and go as I please and to maintain my financial equity in it. But our marriage as such has ended. Full stop.

This dialogue between us continues for the entire three weeks of the tour. As Jane and I zigzag across the country from Perth to Melbourne to Adelaide, back to Brisbane then various regional centres, David and I talk at least once a day. Often several times, because I keep phoning him to try a different angle. To put my case a different way. Sometimes I cry, sometimes I scream, sometimes I can barely speak because of my distress. And in between the calls I am putting on make-up and fixing my hair and dashing out to make appearances, often to hundreds and hundreds of women. I have never had to put on such a brave face and Jane is only too aware of the strain I am under. I can't eat, for a start, because my throat constricts every time I try swallowing. I was already thin when I came back from France, now I am looking gaunt and haggard. I try to cover the dark circles with make-up and hope nobody notices that I am a cot case.

By Adelaide I reach a state of despair. I lie awake one night for hours and decide, irrationally of course, that suicide is probably the only way out of this for me. I get dressed and go looking for the stairs in the hotel, hoping to get up onto the roof. There is no access. The management is obviously aware that sometimes guests have these desperate moments. I tell David how I am feeling and he is horrified. He calls Jane and asks her to watch me every minute of the day which, of course, she can't do. But I realise she is monitoring me pretty closely.

Each day gets more difficult. I am running on automatic pilot. Each time I stand up before an audience to give a talk, I wonder how I am going to get through it. But I do and Jane is always there to whisk me away at the end. To sit and have a late-night drink with me before we collapse into our beds. What a nightmare for her having to prop up this demented writer on tour. Worse than trying to control a drug-crazed rock and roll band. Her friends think she has a cushy life, travelling around the country and staying in plush hotels. If only they knew how difficult her job can be at times, dealing with loopy people. And I'm one of them.

In Canberra I seriously spend time in my hotel room contemplating suicide in a more cool and calculated fashion. Instead of jumping off a building I will organise some tablets and do it properly so there can be no slip-ups. I will organise the legalities to protect our children. I don't want the other woman getting hold of my children's inheritance. Of course this demonstrates how totally irrational I am at the time. There's no way David would allow anything that we had accrued together to go to another person. We had already covered all these possibilities years ago when we made our wills. But I am now seeing the other woman as the enemy and logic and common sense have nothing to do with my reasoning.

That night, neither David nor I get any sleep. I phone him every half-hour, raving incoherently. He lies on our bed at the farm cradling the portable phone in his arms. He is relieved each time I call, no matter what the hour, just because he can hear I am alive.

The last leg of the tour is back in Sydney. David has decided to come down and stay with me at the hotel to lend his support.

He's not doing a turnaround in terms of his stance on our marriage, he just wants to hold my hand for these last few days. He will have to invent a story for the new woman about where he is staying and play the 'mobile phone switched off in the hotel' game again. I feel sorry for him caught between two women, both of whom he obviously loves and cares for. One waiting expectantly for him to launch into a new and exciting relationship; one desperately clinging to him and slipping further and further into a state of insanity.

In Sydney we embrace and David immediately senses my extreme physical and mental frailty. He is very concerned. I have always been the strong one, the doer, the one with endless energy and stamina. Now I am thin and pale and trembling. He makes love to me and I try to pretend that everything is okay. Just like it used to be before all this happened. It's a fantasy in my head, because I know it isn't going to change anything. It's all hopeless.

The next day I have a library talk on the North Shore and we are delighted that some very dear friends have turned up unexpectedly. Two women who were neighbours and close friends when we lived in the Blue Mountains, and also Bob Huber, who was a close colleague of David's from his days working in television. The talk goes well and afterwards we spontaneously join David's old friend Bob for lunch. We have been friends for thirty years and even though we don't see him very often, it's the sort of friendship that picks up exactly where it left off. We chatter and gossip about our children and grandchildren, comparing photographs and funny anecdotes. It's just so warm and familiar and comfortable, and as we sit around the restaurant table I am swamped by the realisation that none of these old relationships will ever be the same again. Here is a friend who has known us as a couple since I was twenty-one, and soon David will have a new partner and the continuity will be broken. Severed. Not that Bob won't still be my friend, of course he will. But there will be an essential shift and I can't help but think of all our friends and extended family members who will be affected in the same way. It just seems too terrible for words.

I sit in silence as we drive back to the hotel. I am feeling angry again. Angry with myself for creating the problem in the first place and angry with David for his part in it. As he drops off the car out the front of the hotel for parking, I take off on foot. Running through the city like a madwoman. I find a corner pub and order a double gin and tonic. I find the darkest corner and sit in it. Fifteen minutes pass and I order another one. Suddenly I see David approaching. He has tracked me down. Unwisely we have a couple more drinks – I haven't been eating properly for weeks and the alcohol affects me much more intensely than usual. David steadies me as we walk back to the hotel. My mind drifts back to Adelaide a week ago when I was on tour. I had a get-together with two female friends who know us both quite well. I poured my heart out to them about our predicament. They listened and expressed great concern. Then one of them said something which at the time seemed a bit outrageous. But now, in my alcohol-dazed state of mind, it seems to make a lot of sense.

'Perhaps what David wants is for you to drag him back from the clutches of this other woman. Like a cavewoman. Club him over the head to knock sense into him and drag him back.'

When we get back to the hotel room, I fly at David in an uncontrolled rage. I whack him around the head a few times then pull back. I pick up various objects and throw them at him.

He's ducking and weaving and trying his best to reason with me. I am, however, completely out of control.

What is happening here? I am re-enacting a thousand domestic brawls I witnessed as a child. My parents at war. Eternally. My mother flying at my father. Scratching at his face and throwing whisky glasses and bottles at him. The only difference is the response. David is totally passive and just defends himself from my wild attack. By this stage my father would have knocked my mother to the floor. She'd have had a black eye, or worse. She may even have been unconscious.

So it has come to this. The final degradation. For my entire adult life I have been non-violent. I have rarely smacked a child on the bottom for bad behaviour. I have always been slow to anger. Tolerant. Docile. Conciliatory. Non-confrontational.

Now here I am like a whirling dervish, attacking David from every angle. Trying to injure him. To knock him down. To bite him and scratch him and maybe even kill him.

Crimes of passion. How most people in our society are murdered. Not by strangers but by those who once loved them.

For the first time ever in my life I truly understand.

I was brought up by parents who were both communists and atheists. I was banned from Sunday school and never crossed the threshold of a church except for a family wedding or funeral. My parents were obsessed by social justice and issues such as human rights. These were the main topics of discussion around our dinner table and if religion, especially Christianity, was mentioned it was usually in a disparaging or negative fashion.

Yet despite her atheism my mother Muriel constantly quoted from the Bible in her everyday conversations, so that although I was never allowed to read 'the good book' I am thoroughly aware of its basic teachings. My parents, in their behaviour towards each other, certainly didn't set a very good example for their children but intellectually the lessons were always there. 'As ye sow, so shall ye reap' was one of my mother's favourites, along with 'Do unto others what you would have them do unto you' and 'Pride comes before a fall'.

These basic precepts have stayed with me all my life and certainly affected the way I brought up my own children. I didn't preach at my children, instead believing that leading by example is the most effective method of parenting. I believe that I demonstrated the importance of kindness and compassion, of love for humanity and of the joys of sharing. I have a firm conviction that the sense of values instilled in a child from birth will stay with them into their adult life. Not if they have been beaten over the head with theories of goodness, but if the theories have been practised as an integral part of their everyday life.

Now my mother's words come back to haunt me. Having believed I was always a kind and compassionate person, I now see myself in a totally different light. And the reason is simple. Instead of putting the welfare and happiness of others in front of my own, I have made a grab for putting my own needs first. I have acted out of self-interest and self-love, and the result of this is laid out before me like a tableau.

It's a complex question. Many would say that I have every right to nurture – or even indulge – myself at this stage of my life. My children have grown up and are successfully independent. They don't really need me the way they did as children. I have worked hard, paid my way and been a 'good' wife and partner to my husband. Loyal and loving and supportive. Well, at least until three years ago.

Others might say that I am getting exactly what I deserve. By wilfully following my own path regardless of the feelings of others, I have lost the right to expect the love and loyalty of my husband any more. Having felt betrayed and rejected, devalued and renounced, he has every right to follow his heart in a new direction.

On reflection, I should have made some difficult decisions in my life several years ago. Intending as I was to launch into an extra-marital affair, I should have made a decision one way or the other. Leave David and go to my lover, knowing full well that the affair would have to end and I would be alone. Or deny my desires and remain faithful to my husband. I should never have imagined that I could have it both ways. That it was possible for me to tip-toe off to France for illicit sex while David unhappily sat back at the farm waiting for me.

I'm sure there is a passage in the Bible that explains all this, but I don't believe it would have helped me to read it. I was hell-bent on doing the things I wanted to do for my own hedonistic reasons. But doing so hasn't made me happy. On the contrary, I have never been so unhappy in all my life. I am undone. Confused and thoroughly miserable. A lost soul, some would say.

46

The book tour has finally finished and David is driving us back to the farm. We haven't discussed my violent outburst of the night before, but we are shaken and subdued. The accumulation of stress, exhaustion from all the travelling and speaking events, the emotional turmoil and the physical effects of not eating properly and drinking to excess have caught up with me. I dare not look in the mirror – not just because I'm having trouble facing myself but because I know I will be alarmed at my deterioration. I just need time to collapse and sleep and eat some home-cooked food and dry out a little. I just need life to be normal for a little while so I can regain my strength for the unhappy times ahead.

When I think about it, my life has been on a razor's edge for most of the year. The lead-up to leaving Australia with a film crew hot on my heels, the difficult time in France, David's discovery of the second affair, his decision to end our marriage, my return to Australia and subsequent discovery of the new woman and then the frenetic book tour. It's no wonder I feel shattered.

We somehow settle into a familiar routine together. He does his calls and paperwork in the morning, then goes into Bathurst to the gym and I stay at home and write and cook and garden. He does the shopping, I do the cooking, and he does the clearing up. We sleep together and hold each other close even though we know it won't be like this for long. After a few days we start to talk again about the bigger issues. I am determined not to get angry or to escalate our conversations into arguments. We must talk it through calmly and rationally. The time for fighting has finished.

I put my case to David very plainly.

'This is how I see it. We have been together for thirty-three years. We love each other and there are still many aspects of our relationship that are worthwhile. Worth hanging on to. We have created, in our time together, a fantastic family. If we split, the family unit will never be the same again. Our children and grandchildren will still love us and we will love them, but the unity will have been destroyed. Then we have our wider family and all our friends, with ties and connections going back three decades and more. Those relationships will never be quite the same again either. Financially, of course, we will both be worse off if our assets are divided. The quality of life that we have worked so hard to create will be severely diminished.

'Then there is our future. I will have to live alone and I certainly don't relish that prospect. You will be in a new relationship, but how will it work? Will you move to South Africa and live there? Will she move here to Australia? She has family and career ties that will make it virtually impossible.

'I believe our marriage is worth fighting for. Let's not give up on it. Please let's give it one more chance. We can work together to rebuild our relationship. I know we can.'

David questions my sincerity. He finds it hard to believe that I am serious, given all that has happened in France over the past few years.

'I was certain you wanted to end our marriage, which is why you were behaving the way you did,' he says. 'I was convinced that there was nothing left for us. I never, ever would have made a commitment to another woman if I believed that there was anything left to salvage. Your reaction has shocked me and now I don't know what to do. I do believe that you love me but I can't stand the thought of going through any more pain. I'm still not convinced that this is what you really want.'

'I didn't realise this was what I wanted either,' I respond. 'It wasn't until I lost you that I realised the terrible mistake I had made.'

During this whole rocky period David hasn't talked about his feelings or his pain with very many people. Not even with his family or closest friends. Only with one woman friend who is also a professional counsellor, and with our nearest neighbours Robert and Sue. But when his brother calls from Sydney I can hear them talking and David is explaining the issues that we have just been discussing. They talk for quite a long time, then David comes back into the family room and sits down quietly.

'He agrees with you,' David says. 'That we would be crazy not to give our relationship another chance. That it would be a mistake to throw it away without at least trying one more time.'

'And what do you think?' I ask

'I think he's probably right.'

I know with absolute certainty that David wouldn't say this if he didn't mean it. He's such a definite person. So black and white. He's obviously made up his mind and he will stick to it. We will have another chance. He won't leave me.

But the look on his face speaks volumes. He's torn because now, somehow, he is going to have to break the news to the new woman. Go back on his promise. Break her heart.

It doesn't make me feel good.

Initially there is little joy in the decision. Instead of feeling elation and a sense of relief, I feel a certain flatness. An anti-climax. Maybe it's because I know David now has to deal with the difficulties of explaining his change of heart to the new woman. Maybe it's because I know I have forced him to make a decision which, although we agree it is the right decision, has been made for practical and pragmatic reasons rather than because he simply adores me and can't live without me. I realise that we will need to work through a tremendous number of problems before we make even the slightest progress in repairing the rift between us. It isn't just a matter of saying, 'Okay, let's stay together' and suddenly being surrounded by a halo of happiness. If it's going to work, it won't be without a lot of struggling and effort from both of us. I wonder if we will make it.

I try to inject some happiness by suggesting that we call the children to share with them our decision. Their reaction is certainly important to me, and I also hope that talking to them may make David feel more positive. One by one we get them on the phone and tell them there's been a resolution. We are staying together. We say there are no guarantees but we are both committed to giving it the best shot we can. One by one, they cry and say how thrilled they are. All they want, they say, is for us to be happy. It's an important decision for them too. Even though they are adults with their own partners and children, deep down they have never lost the child inside. The child that wants his or her parents to stay married. It's only natural.

The question of happiness is on our lips constantly. David believes it will be a long time before he can feel happy again. That so much damage has been done it will take years before he feels confident in me or relaxed in our relationship. I certainly feel happy that a decision has finally been made and that we can move on, but I sense a reserve in David that has never been there before. Almost an indifference.

He has decided not to speak to the new woman immediately but to try and let her down gently. It isn't necessary, however, because she has sensed it in his voice. She simply asks him a direct question about his relationship with me and he confirms it. There has been a reconciliation. After the call he is ashen-faced and will barely speak to me. In fact he becomes withdrawn and stays that way for days and days. I have to stand back and let him go through this, no matter how painful it is for all of us. I have been the spoiler. I have quashed his opportunity for a new and different life and I have put him in a position of having to hurt another person very deeply. Of all the things I have done, this is the one thing that he will probably never, ever forgive me for.

Over the next six weeks, leading up to Christmas, we both have a series of events and conferences to attend in various country towns between Bathurst and southern Queensland. We use the opportunity to catch up with some old friends and there is also talking time, lots of talking time, in the car as we drive over the thousands of kilometres of our journey. It's as though we are recovering from a major illness. We have good days and bad days. He is still emotionally bruised and battered and I am not much better. I yearn for him to be a bit lighter, to be a bit more positive. But he remains subdued and distant. It's going to be a long, slow road to recovery.

We stop making love as frantically as we did during the period when we were, theoretically, 'estranged'. The feeling between us during that phase was so electric that it often resolved itself sexually. Now that a decision has been made, we have slipped back into that 'old married couple' syndrome. Or perhaps it's the numbness David is feeling. Whatever, I hope it will pass and the spark will return.

We are best when we are with other people, especially with good friends who have known us over many years. We don't necessarily discuss everything we have been through with them, but just being together as a couple in the company of those who care about us is reaffirming. We have made the right choice. It will be for the best in the long run.

My preparations leading up to Christmas, however, don't feel as carefree and joyful as usual. Everything seems to be more of an effort, more of a struggle. Christmas has always been a major event in our family life. My brother Jon comes down from the small country town where he has lived for many years and the entire family gathers for two or three days of non-stop present-giving and partying. I don't even have the heart or energy for killing and plucking geese for the table and buy turkey and ham instead. Our mood is more solemn than usual. We still haven't bounced back.

Christmas day, however, is as blissful as ever. The weather is hot, but not unbearably hot, and we eat in the cool of the formal dining room rather than out in the hall as we have done before. After lunch we scatter, with the boys, both large and small, playing cricket on the wide side lawn. I join them as a spectator and Miriam's little Jack Russell terrier, Ulysses, comes and snuggles up to me. Like all terriers, he's bad news around poultry, so we have muzzled him for the day to protect our flocks of geese and ducks. But I feel sorry for him in the heat and remove the muzzle so he can rub his itchy nose on the grass.

I decide to have a late afternoon nap and sleep off the effects of excessive food and wine but am woken to shrieking and general pandemonium. Ulysses has been into the dam after the ducks and has managed to slaughter two of David's favourites. David is running around the garden holding aloft the bleeding birds, shouting in fury and distress. While we are all upset at what has happened, I realise his overreaction is symptomatic of his state of mind. Still very fragile.

People in long-term marriages or partnerships react differently when those relationships come to an end, whether by death or divorce. There is always a period of adjustment and then, for some, a new beginning as life moves on.

When my father died, my mother was initially numb and grief-stricken. She could have seen his death as a way free from the chains of their co-dependent relationship and then made a whole new life for herself. She was only fifty-two at the time, bright and attractive, and could easily have carved out a new career for herself or become involved in a exciting new relationship. She chose not to. She more or less gave up on a life of her own and merged into our family unit instead. Not that there is anything wrong with taking up the role of grandmother, it's just that she stopped having dreams or ambitions of her own and hung her future on her only daughter – me – and her grandchildren instead. She also created a fantasy around the image of her late husband. She somehow forgot all the negative aspects of his personality and reminisced only about the good times they had enjoyed together. It's understandable in many ways that she would want to suppress the painful memories of his infidelities and the subsequent drunken brawling, but sometimes I became very frustrated at the rosy picture she painted of her life with Theo.

I had an aunt who spent her life totally at the beck and call of her husband, who was quite a forceful and dominating character. She was meek and bird-like, but their marriage was happy because they obviously met each other's needs. My uncle didn't like flying in aeroplanes and he had but one favourite holiday destination, to which they returned year after year. They were very set in the pattern of their lives together. When he died, my aunt was initially devastated. But when the shock and grief subsided she decided, despite being well into her eighties, to do a little travelling. It was an amazing thing for her family to behold. Suddenly she was airborne, zipping from Sydney to Broome to Adelaide to Tasmania. Exploring Australia for the first time on her own because during her married life it hadn't been an option. She was a late-life adventurer and for years it was almost impossible to catch her at home.

In France, my friend Margaret Barwick was similarly grief-stricken when her husband David died after a long battle with cancer. Margaret, usually a lively personality, became quiet and almost withdrawn. She slowed down, gained weight and even developed late-onset diabetes. Her friends and family were worried about her. Then something amazing happened. She just took charge of her life again. Picked herself up and went onwards and upwards. She started exercising, kept to a rigid diet and lost weight rapidly. She had always been a keen hands-on gardener and she took to it again with a vengeance, disappearing down the back with barrowloads of plants from early morning until dusk. For several years she had been working on the manuscript for an encyclopaedia of tropical trees, her particular passion. She and David had spent their married life in tropical regions of the world, where he had been a colonial governor. During this phase of their life she had developed her passion for plants and had helped establish botanic gardens and parks in several of their postings. With her renewed energy and fitness she finished the manuscript, found an English publisher and worked day and night to prepare the large volume for publication. She was a dynamo.

So there is life after a long-term marriage ends. There can be a new beginning. My problem is I just can't imagine what my life would be like without David. It would be like a death, I guess. Even though we have had major ups and downs and at times I have felt a desperate need to escape from the confines of our relationship, in truth I can't visualise myself as a single woman. I feel as though our lives are bound together through more than just love. Through myriad connections and shared experiences. Some people say that choosing divorce is the 'easy way out' of a troubled marriage. To me it feels as though it's the most difficult way out. Surely staying together and trying to work things out is an easier solution. For me, anyway.

49

Having moved from Leura to the farm at Yetholme to be closer to Miriam and her growing family in Bathurst, it was inevitable that they would move away. It somehow never works, the notion of trailing after your adult children in the hope of being involved and useful grandparents. Some young families move back to be near their parents for mutual support as the grandchildren grow up and the grandparents age. Certainly that's why Miriam and Rick moved from Canberra to the Blue Mountains nine years ago. But when their dreams and careers take them further afield there is little point in following in their wake, because there is no assurance that they won't keep moving on.

It took Miriam a few weeks to pluck up the courage to tell me about the family's proposed move to Adelaide. She had completed her communications degree in Canberra the same year Eamonn (now ten) was born, and also part of a law degree. She and we always assumed that at some stage she'd go back and finish the law component of the degree. The year she became pregnant with Gus, her youngest son, she'd been accepted into law as an external student. She knew it would be difficult, juggling several years of university with three small children, but she was excited at the prospect of getting her brain into gear again. Then she discovered she was expecting a fourth child and the prospect of studying even part-time became an impossibility.

When Gus was two years old, Miriam started looking again for possible post-graduate courses to undertake as an external student. One day by chance she stumbled across a fairly radical course that fired her imagination and completely changed the direction of her future career. The Bachelor of Midwifery is a relatively new course offered by Flinders University in Adelaide and is one of only a few available in Australia. Instead of midwifery being an additional qualification to general nursing, this degree stands alone. The few students accepted each year are trained to be an elite group of highly qualified practitioners capable of providing care in birth centres, hospitals or at home. One aim is to fill the gap in remote and rural areas, where obstetricians don't choose to practice, by providing specialist midwives, which will enable women to have their babies close to home rather than travelling to hospitals in larger towns or cities.

Miriam had given birth to three of her four sons at home with midwives, one in Canberra and two in Katoomba. During her first pregnancy she read extensively on the subject of birth and as a result of her research decided that homebirth was, from her perspective, safer and preferable. The only reason Gus, the last born, emerged in a hospital delivery suite was because there were no independent midwives practising in Bathurst at the time and because the family was too broke at that stage to afford the costs involved. Homebirth midwives currently have no access to insurance and their charges cannot be recouped through

Medicare, so people wanting to have a baby at home need to set aside several thousand dollars to cover these expenses.

I had also had a homebirth – my last child, Ethan – and Miriam had been reared in a family that considered birth a normal part of life rather than a medical condition. Over the decade in which she produced her children, regular contact with homebirth midwives had politicised Miriam about the government's attitude to birth alternatives. This course would not only allow Miriam to gain a high level of expertise in an area she felt passionately about, but would also put her into a position of being able to lobby for a better deal both for midwives and for expecting parents. She was ecstatic at the possibility of doing the course and applied immediately, hoping that her previous degree and her experiences of natural birth would stand her in good stead for being accepted.

Although I was thrilled that Miriam had stumbled across a career path for which she seemed destined, I was also devastated at the prospect of losing her and her family to Adelaide. While they were living in Bathurst I saw them regularly, usually several times during the week when I would pick the boys up after school or meet Miriam during the day, and certainly every weekend for a big day at the farm and Sunday lunch. It had become a tradition. Now I would be lucky to see them once or twice a year, and the close bond I had developed with the four small boys would be severed, temporarily at least. I was also concerned that this situation would add pressure to my relationship with David. When all the family is around it somehow diffuses the one-on-one relationship that couples face when children have grown up and left home. Our son Aaron and his family live at Mudgee, just an hour and a half away, but he is often on call in his job and can't get over to the farm at the weekends. We just don't have as much regular contact with these grandchildren as we do with Miriam's boys.

The move to Adelaide was not without its problems. Miriam applied for the course but wouldn't find out if she had been accepted until after Christmas, giving her just a few short weeks to sell the house, pack up and move. Not to mention the problem of Rick finding a new job or getting a transfer from his office in Bathurst.

It's very difficult to prepare a house for selling when there are four small boys around. As fast as Miriam tidies up or renovates an area of the house or garden, the boys blunder along and make a mess of it. I bring them out to the farm for days at a time to try to give her a clear run at getting the place looking as good as possible. At exactly the moment they choose to put their house on the market, the bottom falls out of real estate. One week their neighbours sell their property for an excellent price and two weeks later Miriam and Rick's estate agents can't even get a prospective buyer through the door for an inspection. By mid-January Miriam is beside herself with anxiety. They realise they will have to rent out the Bathurst house and rent a place in Adelaide, at least for the first six months. Rick has been applying for transfers but without success.

Finally word comes through that she has been accepted into the course. One of only twenty-five students out of several hundred applicants. While delighted with the news, she knows it's crunch time. Deferment is not an option.

'Go,' I say to her. 'Throw the boys in the car and we'll pay for a motel until you find a place to live. Just get yourselves down there and we'll look after the rest. Rick can stay until you find a place, then he and I will pack everything up and send it across to you. He can follow.'

So that's exactly what happened. Miriam bravely drove with the four boys across the Hay Plains, car packed to the gunnels. They had been to Adelaide briefly the previous year to check it out, so she had already found a good caravan park near the beach with comfortable air-conditioned cabins. It was a two-day drive and they were all totally exhausted when they finally limped into the caravan park. The boys were in holiday mood, being so near the beach, but for Miriam it was anything but a relaxing period. She spent weeks dashing from one real estate agent to another looking for a house to rent. It was almost impossible to find a suitable house within their limited budget that was also big enough for a family of six. Then there were the animals – two cats and two dogs. The agents all shook their heads.

Her phone calls home became increasingly more frantic.

'Don't worry, don't worry,' I reassured her. 'We'll keep the cats here at the farm with us and find a home for Lippy [the larger of the dogs]. Surely you'll be allowed to keep Ulysses; he's such a cute little dog.'

So she went back to the agencies and eventually found a place that would allow one pet only. She enrolled the three older boys in a local school and managed to get a part-time place for Gus at the university child care centre. Rick and I packed up the Bathurst house and ordered a removalist van. For the last week he stayed alone at the house, camping on a single bed mattress, until news came through that his work had managed to organise a transfer. Such a huge relief. He packed Ulysses and their last few possessions in the second car and headed south, leaving a large gap in our lives.

50

It's now more than a year since David and I made our decision to stay together. It's been a rocky fifteen months but we have somehow survived and most of the time things seem to be okay. We have both made compromises and have talked and talked about the past, about the present and about the future. In some ways this massive shake-up has been good for our relationship. We have had to take a step back and examine ourselves and each other more vigorously than many people do in their entire lives. We have learned a lot about each other and a lot about ourselves. We have laughed and cried and continued to argue at times, but mostly in a constructive rather than in a destructive or negative manner.

There are still stumbling blocks and things that worry both of us. For me it is the fear that David will never really be able to forgive me for what happened over those three summers in France. Inevitably, whenever we argue, my love affairs somehow become part of the conversation. Every time David is moved to anger – no matter what the issue may be – the subject of my infidelity crops up and at those moments my heart sinks. Is it always going to be there like a dark shadow lurking in the background of our lives? No matter how much we move on, we can't seem to shake it off. During one long-distance phone conversation, when we are both getting upset about a communication problem, he suddenly says, 'How do you expect me to feel? You broke my heart.'

I know I did and I fear he may never recover.

On the other hand, David's worry is that I am bored with our relationship. Even though he knows I love him, he is also aware that I crave more excitement in my life than he does. There is an element of truth in this, of course, and it's a common problem in long-term relationships. I spent three decades of my life holding the fort at home while he had an exciting and adventurous career as a filmmaker. Now he is happy to spend a lot more time at home and I am raring to get up and go.

Because these personal issues are always on my mind, I listen intently to television and radio programs that touch on any issues concerning relationships. I also read extensively on the subject, groping for a better understanding. On an English science program, the physical manifestations of sexual attraction are pinpointed. After extensive study and testing they have discovered that when humans feel sexual attraction to another person endorphins are released, just as they are when people exercise vigorously. It's a 'feel good' sensation and it's also highly addictive, which explains why humans just love to fall in love. It's such an exciting feeling. When I make love to David, it is more deeply sexually satisfying than with either of my lovers, so he finds it difficult to understand why I would therefore be unfaithful to him. All I can say is that it must be the excitement factor. The tingling thrill of a new relationship. And I have learned, the hard way, that the downside is more painful than the tingling thrill is worth.

On the car radio one day I hear an interview with a so-called 'expert' on family relationships who has been compiling statistics on modern marriages. According to his findings, people of my generation – the baby boomers – have three major life partner-ships. Three long-term relationships or marriages. The first occurs in late teens or early twenties. First love. It's a carefree, fun relationship that involves a lot of partying and travelling and good times. In our late twenties or early thirties, the second rela-tionship takes over. It's a more serious and settled partnership in which the couple set up home and possibly start a family. It lasts for fifteen to twenty years. The third relationship occurs in our forties or fifties, and the partner chosen is a soul mate. A rela-tionship based on shared passions and perspectives. Sex is less important, according to the statistics, than mutual interests.

In essence the expert is saying that we no longer expect to have a life-long partner. We aspire to three satisfying relation-ships that are successful at various times of our lives according to our needs and our expectations. First playmate, next housemate, finally soul mate. I'm not convinced we can parcel our lives up into such tidy, well-thought-out packages. That we can throw over one partner because the time has come to move on. That we can cut and run because we have outgrown our earlier relationships. If it was that easy we would all be statistics.

Another friend, a professional marriage guidance counsellor, tells me that the number of women leaving their husbands after twenty-five or thirty years of marriage is rapidly on the increase. Just when relationships should be reaching that comfortable, easy stage they are falling apart. Women are initiating the change, not men. I listen and understand how these situations can so easily happen. It's quite frightening. When David says he no longer recognises me as the same woman he has lived with for more than thirty years, I totally understand. I don't feel like the same woman, and in many ways I am simply not her any more. I have spent a lot of time agonising about it and trying to understand myself and who I have become. Trying to understand how all this happened to me, and why I reacted in the way that I did.

To be honest, a lot of it I don't understand. I can only assume that for the past four years I have been on some sort of journey, spiritual as much as physical and emotional. It's a side of myself that I normally deny – that I could possibly have a 'spiritual' aspect to my personality. But I must acknowledge that I've been searching for something, trying to find myself and gain some insight along the way. My whole adult life has been filled with people and responsibilities – my husband, my children, my mother, my career, my grandchildren. I ran away from all of that because I wanted time to myself. To be alone. But I did not achieve that goal – in fact I ended up crowding my life with even more people and responsibilities, and in doing so created confusion, conflict and contradiction.

On one level, I realise that I probably did want to end my relationship with David and just be my own person. Live independently, travel as I choose and make all my own decisions. But when it came to the crunch, when I pushed my relationship with him to the brink and he was poised to leave me, I relented. I panicked. I was terrified of abandonment and, ultimately, of being alone. He thinks I only wanted to stay with him because of my desperate desire to hold together our wonderful family unit.

That is part of it, of course, but by no means is it the whole story. I obviously have a tremendous need for David in my life – a dependency – and this need probably goes back to my difficult childhood. A fear of abandonment. A little girl lost. Who knows? It would probably take years of therapy or analysis to figure it all out and make some sense of it.

All I do know is that I want to feel comfortable with myself again. To feel content and at peace. And I haven't reached that stage, no matter how hard I have tried. No matter how hard we have *both* tried.

David and I still have many obstacles to overcome, the main one being the house in the village in France. During the period I was convincing David that we shouldn't separate, the question of the house came up as a major sticking point. David was adamant he has no desire to ever visit the house or the village again because what happened there has spoiled that region of France for him for ever. At that difficult stage I was prepared to do anything, even sell the house, to keep us together. I made the point that our marriage was more important than a house. Which of course it is.

But when I returned in April 2004 to lead another walking tour, I was filled with regret at the thought of leaving this place forever. Indeed we both reneged on words spoken during that tumultuous period. Although David insisted he could never return, he did in fact join me in Frayssinet in late May after the Cannes Film Festival. Just as he had done the year before. The summer of the devastating heatwave. This time I hoped he might start to feel better about this place. It was a vain hope.

Something happens to me when I turn the big brass key in the old mortice lock and swing open the door into the main room of that little house. It feels as though something in the walls envelops me and makes me at one with it, part of a continuum of people who have lived under this old roof for centuries. I have no idea what comes over me when I arrive but I know I will feel tremendous loss if I have to leave and never return. In many respects the house symbolises a stage of my life that was very important to me. My moment of freedom and escape. My taste of recklessness and irresponsibility. My experiment at dipping a toe into another culture and finding myself feeling totally at home in a foreign land.

Momentous for me. Totally destructive for David.

At least that year we had a positive reason to be together at the house. After the walking tour we spent the entire month of June filming a documentary for SBS television about the one-hundredth anniversary of Madame Murat's restaurant. I have loved this establishment since I first came to France four years ago, and last year I discovered that they were planning a big party to celebrate the fact that the restaurant has been in the same family for a century. Five generations of women have owned and operated what is essentially a simple country kitchen that caters mainly to working men – construction and road workers, the men from the local quarry and veal farm, the truck drivers and local tradesmen. Having made friends with Jeanette (Madame Murat) and her daughter Sylvie, who are the current proprietors, I thought it would make an inspirational film, showing a slice of traditional life that is rapidly disappearing all over the French countryside. So I spent some time researching the idea with the Murat family, looking back at their old photographs and archives and studying the cuisine from when the restaurant first opened in 1904.

I had high hopes that making the film together would be such a positive experience it might help David overcome his aversion to the place. I believed if we could work together closely with a common goal – to make the best possible film about something we both felt strongly committed to – it would not only be good for our relationship, it might just help make David feel he could regard the house as 'his' again.

Sadly, it was not to be. While we were making the film we were certainly united in our passion for the project and it was a great experience. But the moment it ended and we packed up the house to come back to Australia, David made it quite clear that this would be his last visit. That he had only come to help with the film and felt no differently about the place than he had the previous year. For him it has been a place of such pain and sadness that he simply doesn't want to relive it year after year. The house, in fact, has become the symbol of our troubled marriage and it comes between us like a wedge. I am irresistibly drawn to it and he is overwhelmingly repelled by it, and until we resolve the issue of whether we should keep the house or sell it our marriage will remain shaky.

So we have reached an impasse. My yearning for the house in the village and the freedom to spend some time there alone each year now seems to be an impossible dream. I acknowledge that the situation is of my own making but it doesn't make it any easier to resolve. Running away from the scene of the crime won't solve the original problem, either. The problem of David and me rebuilding our marriage and our relationship. Even if we found a house in another part of France we would be taking our problem with us, not leaving it behind in Frayssinet.

51

Lynne's pregnancy this time around is totally different from the one she experienced when carrying Isabella. Although slightly nauseous during the first few weeks, she has been feeling strong and healthy and has also been gaining a good amount of weight. With Isabella her belly remained very small and neat right until the end. This time, four months before she is due, her tummy is much larger than she was when full-term last time round. It's very encouraging.

During the pregnancy Lynne has had all the usual tests but she and Ethan have decided to avoid any invasive testing to determine if this new baby has a genetic problem. Apart from the fact that there is an element of risk attached to all these tests – a chance of miscarriage – their attitude is that they will be proceeding with the pregnancy no matter what the outcome. So there is no point testing for abnormalities if there is no plan to consider a termination should the new baby have any problems. They are also keen for the sex of the baby to be a surprise. They are very clear about their decision and are upset several times when the genetic counsellors try to pressure them into having precautionary tests done. They stick to their guns, however, and also decide to have a homebirth this time, much to the surprise and dismay of various doctors who are caring for Isabella.

Miriam was Lynne and Ethan's supporter when Isabella was born in the local hospital, but now she is living in Adelaide she won't be around to help. So they ask if I will come along and help, and I am absolutely thrilled. I have been at the births of Miriam's four boys, but I have never had an expectation that my daughters-in-law would want me to be around while they were in labour. It will be an amazing experience.

Towards the end of her pregnancy, Lynne is huge and her belly looks hilariously out of proportion to her tiny, thin-hipped body. We look back at photographs taken just before Isabella was born and we can't help but laugh. This time she looks twice the size and her tummy skin is stretched tight like a drum around the active lump that is the unborn child. I go with her for an ante-natal visit to meet the midwife, who is Dutch, very practical and down-to-earth. We establish a good rapport and talk about various options for the birth. Lynne likes the idea of spending time in the bath during labour. She has also asked her sister Bronwyn to come and help. The plan is for Lynne's mother to come and pick up Isabella immediately Lynne goes into labour, so that Lynne can totally relax and focus on the birth. If Isabella is in the house, especially if she gets grizzly or unhappy, Lynne will be concerned and distracted. I think it's an excellent idea.

In the weeks leading up to the due date, Lynne goes in and out of labour several times. I drive back and forth between the farm and Katoomba and also stay over several nights because

Lynne feels certain the birth is imminent. But every time it looks as though she's about to pop, it all fades away.

When I stay overnight I share a room with Isabella and tend to her night-time needs. She is hooked up to a pump that delivers formula directly into her belly every two hours. The pump releases formula continuously at a slow rate overnight, but gases build up in her stomach as the food is digested. While I do know a little about the complexities of Isabella's care regime, it isn't until I am looking after her myself that I appreciate just how demanding it is for Ethan and Lynne. I need to set my alarm to wake up twice during the night so I can 'de-gas' her little tummy. It involves disconnecting the pump, closing off the tubes then lowering the belly tube so that excess gas can escape from inside her tummy. The whole system then has to be flushed with sterile water and reconnected. Needless to say it can't be done while half asleep. I have to wake myself up totally so that I can pay attention to what I am doing. It's quite exhausting. Then before dawn I have to wake up again and give Isabella a suppository because otherwise her bowels won't work and, again, she will be in pain and distress. My admiration for my son and his young partner soars as I fully comprehend the breadth of their responsibilities.

When Lynne reaches seven days overdue, the midwife comes for a meeting at their little house. All the indications are that she is ripe and ready to go but something is stopping the process. We are all aware that there will be a certain level of fear around this birth. Even though the doctor and the midwife are confident the unborn child is perfectly normal and healthy, it's not unusual for women who have had a problem with a previous birth to become 'blocked'. The apprehension affects nature's ability to trigger the labour.

It's a positive session and we talk honestly and openly. One of the best aspects of having a homebirth is the relationship that develops between the mother and the midwife that then spills over to the whole family, the father and the birth supporters. It is just so much more personal and intimate than having a baby in a hospital with whoever happens to be on duty at the time. Lynne has a good cry, which also helps. She knows that if she goes much more overdue she may not be able to stay at home for the birth. So the pressure is on.

Naturally, now that we have talked through the fears, Lynne goes spontaneously into labour. Weeks ago I made a large pot of chicken soup and it's on standby in the freezer. All is in readiness. Bronwyn arrives and Lynne's mother, Glynnis, takes Isabella and all her medical paraphernalia and toys and leaves us to get on with the birth peacefully.

Lynne is the most organised person I know. A place for everything and everything in its place. We light a fire because it's early March and already quite cold in the mountains. We are conserving hot water in case she feels like soaking in a bath and we are trying to keep the atmosphere as calm and soothing as possible. For the first few hours she happily labours alone. Bronwyn, the midwife and I chat quietly and keep an eye on her, knowing she will call us to her side when she really needs us. By early afternoon she does and we take turns to apply hot packs to her back and abdomen and to rock her through the contractions, which are becoming stronger and stronger. It's obviously quite a big baby and Lynne is such a small person – probably about a size 8 – and because Isabella was so tiny this time is a bit like a first birth. Her pelvic bones will have to open up really wide to get this baby out.

Ethan is, as ever, strong and unfazed. He has been to many births because when he was a child I sometimes went to support friends having homebirths and he loved to come along. He also attended three of his sister's labours. So he knows exactly what to expect. I am proud of his resilient character and his composure. Lynne is also totally in control. Every fibre of her small body is focused on the task at hand and she works well with the midwife, relaxing and breathing and following her instincts. Eventually, after a very long and hard first stage, she is ready to push. And what a task it is. Bronwyn and I catch a glimpse of the baby's head as Lynne bears down with tremendous effort. It's a big, big head and somehow Lynne has to push it through. Yet not for a moment do we lose confidence.

Each contraction brings the head further and further down and although we can see that it's a monumental task, Lynne is surely up to it. Ethan has been supporting Lynne by holding her weight in his arms while sitting on the edge of their bed. Now he moves around to the other end and Bronwyn takes over his position. As the head starts to crown the midwife takes a back seat, encouraging Ethan to work with Lynne delivering their own child. To catch the baby. I'm supporting Lynne's weight too and have a perfect view of what's happening, blurred by the tears that are falling from my eyes.

Suddenly the baby's head emerges and Ethan cradles it in the palm of his hand. The midwife checks to make sure the cord is not around the baby's neck and also positions the shoulders. On the next push the baby's body slides gently out, held lovingly in Ethan's cupped hands. He passes the baby between Lynne's legs and into her arms. They huddle together to discover the sex. It's a boy. A very big boy, and he's pink and wide awake and filling his eager lungs with his first breath of air. At a glance it is obvious he is perfectly healthy and normal. And lusty and hungry like most newborn babies.

Caius Atticus is the name they have chosen. Quite a mouthful, but distinctive. He looks a lot like his Sicilian grandfather.

An hour after the birth David arrives, flushed with excitement, to greet his new grandson. We sit together at the end of the bed and gaze at Caius adoringly, so relieved that he is the perfect baby his parents so desperately wanted.

His birth has had a profound effect on me and I believe on David as well. It's as though Caius has brought with him new hope and new love. A new beginning. For Ethan, Lynne and Isabella. And hopefully for David and me.

MORE BESTSELLING NON-FICTION AVAILABLE FROM PAN MACMILLAN

Mary Moody
Au Revoir: Running away from home at fifty

Living the good life in the Blue Mountains in New South Wales with her husband, four grown-up children and four (and counting) grandchildren, Mary Moody's life was full. At fifty, she had built a satisfying career as a writer and television presenter which allowed her time to look after her family, house and garden. The only thing missing was time for herself, a chance to reflect on life and its meaning. Like many women of her generation, caught up with the commitments of work and family, Mary had never had a moment alone – so she decided to say *au revoir*. She ran away to live on her own for six glorious months in the rural paradise of south-west France.

Au Revoir is the story of Mary's solo journey. It is funny, warm and reflective, as Mary adapts to life as a single person in The Lot, one of the most remote and beautiful parts of France. Revelling in the food, seasons and characters she encountered, Mary gained new insight into herself while enjoying life to the full. Her account of an escape – with its exhilarating freedom, new experiences and chance for renewal – will inspire every reader to run away from home.

Mary Moody
Last Tango in Toulouse: Torn between two loves

The year of her fiftieth birthday, gardening writer Mary Moody ran away from home, family and work for six months to live in a remote French village. Her book about these experiences, *Au Revoir*, struck a chord with tens of thousands of readers across Australia. Yet those experiences were to mark a beginning rather than an end. They were six months that turned the rest of her life upside down, as she bought a house in the village, persuaded her husband to sell the family home of twenty-five years and take up goose farming in central New South Wales, and abandoned her television career in favour of writing about her travelling experiences.

Yet even these dramatic events were merely the outward signs of far deeper changes that challenged the stability of thirty years of monogamy and motherhood. To her surprise, Mary found herself grappling with the intense emotion of an affair, and its consequences for her marriage and family. Her account of this fraught subject is frank, honest and painful, just as her and her husband's response to it is moving and inspirational. Amid this turmoil, Mary also rediscovered a sister not seen by the family for nearly fifty years. *Last Tango in Toulouse* is Mary's compelling account of these tumultuous upheavals in her life, and an affirmation of the power of family in overcoming the greatest challenges. Written with humour, warmth and passion, and an often searing honesty, *Last Tango in Toulouse* shows that life really can begin again at 50.